Regular Guys

34 Years Beyond Adolescence

Regular Guys

34 Years Beyond Adolescence

DANIEL OFFER

Northwestern University
Chicago, Illinois

MARJORIE KAIZ OFFER

Northwestern University
Chicago, Illinois

and

ERIC OSTROV

Private Practice
Chicago, Illinois

KLUWER ACADEMIC/PLENUM PUBLISHERS
NEW YORK, BOSTON, DORDRECHT, LONDON, MOSCOW

Library of Congress Cataloging-in-Publication Data

Offer, Daniel.
    Regular guys : 34 years beyond adolescence / by Daniel Offer, Marjorie Kaiz Offer, and
Eric Ostrov.
        p.   cm.
    Includes bibliographical references (p.) and index.
    ISBN 0-306-48585-0
    1. Middle aged men–Psychology–Longitudinal studies.   I. Offer, Marjorie Kaiz.   II.
Ostrov, Eric, 1941–   III. Title.

BF692.5.O34 2004
155.6'6'081–dc22   2004042178

ISBN 0-306-48548-6

© 2004 by Kluwer Academic/Plenum Publishers, New York
233 Spring Street, New York, New York 10013

http://www.kluweronline.com

10 9 8 7 6 5 4 3 2 1

A C.I.P. record for this book is available from the Library of Congress.

Permissions for books published in Europe: permissions@wkap.nl
Permissions for books published in the United States of America: permissions@wkap.com

Printed in the United States of America

To Kenneth I. Howard
Happy the man who finds a generous friend
Greek Proverb

To Seymour P. Kaiz, M.D. and Ruth Jacobson Kaiz
who always believed it could be done

À mi esposa y todos mis niños con amor
hasta siempre

Acknowledgments

Completing any scholarly study requires the help of many colleagues, friends, and family. Since the adulthood phase of the Offer Longitudinal Study was primarily self-funded by the senior and second author, supportive expertise was given, for the most part, pro bono. Our gratitude to those who contributed their skills is indescribable. At every step of the project, these persons gave with a generosity that is unmatched in our experience.

We received expert consultation in each phase of this study from the late Kenneth I. Howard, Professor of Psychology, Northwestern University and the Patricia M. Nielsen Research Chair, The Family Institute at Northwestern University. He was with the project from its inception in 1963. The sharing of his time, intellect, and resources during an 11-year period of this study made this entire endeavor possible. We miss him profoundly.

Of great assistance to us was a three-year research grant from Thomas F. Pick of Northfield, Illinois. His investment in our efforts gave us enormous affirmation and allowed us to continue with enhanced confidence. We shall always be grateful for this gift.

We are deeply indebted to the late Judith Baskin Offer and Melvin Sabshin whose contributions to the first two books in this study, *The Psychological World of the Teenager* and *From Teenage to Young Manhood*, gave us a bedrock on which to build this scientific undertaking.

We have been greatly helped throughout this research project by people whose special talents made all the difference. We wish to thank Michael Susman of Henry R. Ferris & Company, who helped locate the most difficult-to-find subjects; and Marge Deitelbaum Jaffe, who contributed to the search for the subjects. We are indebted to Susan Taber, Regina Casper, the late Andrew Boxer, Dan P. McAdams and Charles B. Strozier for help in development and the critique of the interview instrument.

We are grateful to Susan Tabor, Janet Shiff, Larry Shiff, Judith Marshal Jobbitt, Thomas Marshall, Mark Epperson, Allan S. Cohen, and George Franklin for participation in the testing of this instrument. We want to give special thanks to Susan Taber who generously traveled the U.S. interviewing many of the subjects. Her contribution was immeasurable and invaluable.

During our travels around the U.S. to interview subjects, we were aided by Pamela Tremayne, Atlanta, Georgia; Sally Allen, the Gary-Williams Energy Corporation, Denver, Colorado; Maria Boyd, the Upland Public Library, Upland, California; Ruth and Allan Schacter, Pittsburgh, Pennsylvania; Susan Frank, Michigan State University, East Lansing, Michigan; Mark A. Wellek of Phoenix, Arizona; Eileen Higgins, the Glen Ellyn Public Library, Glen Ellyn, Illinois; the Northwest Branch of the Tampa Public Library, Tampa Florida; Nancy and Dicran Goulian, New York City; Marsha Slomowitz, Northwestern University Medical School, Chicago, Illinois; Carol Davis and Sandy Hazen, the American Psychiatric Association, Washington, D. C.; and Mary and Morry Joftus, St. Louis, Missouri.

The transcriptions of the interviews could not have been completed without the talents of Lucina Gallagher and Jerry Kayne.

We are indebted to Bruce Brisco for supervising with the data entry and the generation of the frequency counts. In addition, he was responsible for all the computer services for the entire project including the statistical analysis. His understanding of the study and its organization was invaluable. He was always there when we needed him.

We thank Zoran Martinovich of Northwestern University for his aid in the statistical analysis as well as support with the tables and figures. Also providing thoughtful computer support was Al Erlebacher and Josh Mangoubi. Sari Landsman Knight, an intern, provided insight during the first analysis of the subjects in the three routes.

We want to say a special thank you to staff members of Northwestern University who have been so helpful. Sandra Downey has been wonderfully supportive in preparing this manuscript. We owe a debt of gratitude to Elizabeth Crown of University Relations who has helped bring the study to the attention of both the health sciences and general community worldwide.

We have been helped in the writing of this book by three talented colleagues: Cybelle Weisser, whose writing gift has allowed us to tell the compelling story of three subjects in a most interesting way; Emily Bennett, whose contribution to the chapter on the overview of the literature in this book was most helpful; and David Albert, who provided the background for the family constellation literature review.

Throughout the 13 years it took to complete this research project and subsequent book, there were several people who continuously provided support, suggestions, and confidence. First among those are our children Raphael E. Offer,

Susan Offer Szafir, and Tamar Offer Yehoshua. A special thank you for all those years of listening. Friends also provided wise consul and advice including Sue Pick, Ivan Dee, Barbara Burgess, Marcine Weiner, Arthur Weiner, Margaret Schaffer, Peter Barglow, Jan Smith, Elaine Trikolas Kisisel, Suzanne Grais Hammond, Carol Tavis, and Jane Davis. A special thank you to Gerald H. Kaiz.

And for the 67 men who participated in the middle-age phase of the Offer Longitudinal Study, we feel gratitude, admiration, and affection. Thank you for sharing your lives with us over 34 years. Your willingness to continue to participate in this phase of the story is historically unprecedented. It allowed for a subject follow-up rate (94%) over a 34-year period that has not been matched in psychiatric or psychological longitudinal research in the 20th century. We salute you, our regular guys.

There was never yet an uninteresting life.
Such a thing is an impossibility.
Inside the dullest exterior there is a drama, a comedy, and a tragedy.

—*Mark (Samuel Clemens) Twain*

Contents

Chapter 1

Introduction

This book presents a study of a group of normal men moving from adolescence to middle age. In their teenage years these men were studied as part of a quest to further understand normal adolescent functioning, which then, and to this day, is the subject of much academic dispute and misunderstanding. A bridge is drawn in this book between the in-depth study of these subjects as teenagers and their functioning decades later, when they were in their late 40's. This bridge enriches the study of both phases of life and explicates, to an extent never before found in the literature, the extrapolation of normality in adolescence into adulthood after a span of 34 years.

Every person has taken, or must anticipate taking, the journey from adolescence to middle age. This journey takes us from the incipiency, the unworldliness, the inchoateness of youth to the realization, and, hopefully, gratification of a life largely formed. It takes us from the promise and tenuousness of the teenage years to the immutability of what has been, with a reaching toward crescendo and repose. This book helps answer the question: Where will we be in late middle age, given who and what we were as teenagers?

From 1958 through 1961, the senior author (Daniel Offer) was a resident at Michael Reese Hospital and Medical Center, Chicago, Illinois. In those years, the psychiatric training program was one of the best in the USA. The hospital began in 1881 as a teaching institution. For many years, it was a leader in research in medicine. Among the medical pioneers who practiced there were: Dr. J. Hess who invented the incubator for premature infants in 1915; Dr. Necheles who designed and constructed the first artificial kidney machine in 1920; Drs. Saskil and R. Levine who made significant contributions to the cause and treatment of diabetes; and Dr. R. Grinker who was a pioneer in psychosomatic studies in psychiatry.

1

In the 1950's and 1960's, the Medical Center had 120 full time researchers and educators. The residency programs in all major disciplines were outstanding. Michael Reese Hospital was known nationally as a leader in psychiatry, medicine, surgery, pediatrics, and OB-Gyne.

To be a psychiatric resident at Michael Reese in the late 1950's and early 1960's was an exciting experience. There was an interest in adolescent psychiatry, but, as was true throughout the United States, the field was nascent, and had just begun to develop a separate identity or viable institutions. In 1958, the American Society for Adolescent Psychiatry was founded, devoted exclusively to the treatment and study of adolescence. The Society of Adolescent Medicine (S.A.M.) was founded in 1968. In 1984, the Society for Research in Adolescence was founded. It was not until 1986 that the American Academy of Child Psychiatry added the word "adolescent" to their name. The sub-board in adolescent medicine was first given in 1994 for pediatricians and internists.

In the late 1950's, the gold standard for psychiatric theory and practice was psychoanalysis. All five leading centers of psychiatry in the Chicago area, for instance, were chaired by psychoanalysts. Long-term, psychoanalytically oriented treatment facilities such as the Menninger Clinic, Chestnut Lodge, and Austin Riggs were viewed as the best treatment facilities psychiatry had to offer. To advance in psychiatry, one had to undergo a personal psychoanalysis and to complete a candidacy in the local psychoanalytic institute.

Following Freud's examples, psychiatry assumed the best way to understand humans in general was to study the pathological, the deviant, the abnormal. As a case in point, Freud's theory of the Oedipus Complex was based on the study of Little Hans, a child with a phobia toward horses. His writing on adolescents was exemplified by Dora, a troubled hysteric. His daughter Anna studied children in war-torn England. In the German tradition of grand theories that try to explain everything, psychoanalysis was looked to for an explanation of far-reaching phenomena including the origins of war and the deeper meaning of works of literature. Theories of normal adolescence sprung from such grand theories, and various theorists wrote at length and authoritatively about adolescence although they had never studied them as a group. While there was some interest in adolescence, very few empirical studies had been done. Douvan and Adelson's (1966) and Masterson's (1967) books were contemplated but not yet written.

In the 1960's, psychiatry's emphasis continued to be on the abnormal, which put it in the awkward position of saying people were abnormal while having only a vague notion of what was normal, the very standard one would imagine abnormal would be measured against. Offer and Sabshin (1966, 1984, 1991) wrote extensively about this issue, describing and hoping to remedy the conceptual confusion as well as a dearth of empirical data in the field of psychiatry about what constituted normality.

Against this background, the research that forms the basis for this book began. An incident involving hospitalized teens at Michael Reese inspired this work. A group of these teens pulled a fire alarm. Within minutes, the police and the fire department arrived. When the teens observed them go into the hospital, they ran out and stole a police car, which they drove through the streets of Chicago with lights flashing and sirens sounding. When they ran out of gas, they abandoned the car and returned to the hospital using public transportation. The police were so embarrassed that they did not press charges. The Director of Residency Training held a conference to discuss the incident. The major question discussed was whether this was a normal adolescent prank or was a manifestation of these teens' emotional disturbance. The staff could not agree and the question was left unresolved. It occurred to the senior author that the discussion at the conference was largely informed by speculation or personal experience. There was no robust body of literature on the subject of normal adolescence to fall back on for guidance.

The senior author decided to study normal adolescents and learn through empirical investigation, without sacrificing depth of understanding, what being a normal adolescent entails.

This methodology contrasts with a dominant position of psychiatry at the time, that a true understanding of a person could only come from listening to and observing them for years "on the couch," i.e. through the use of psychoanalysis. It is evident that the number of subjects that can be so studied is quite limited, not to mention that usually the only persons who would be available for such study would be patients seeking help or mental health professionals trying to become analysts. Clearly, studies using only such subjects are skewed toward studying pathological not normal persons.

What the senior author did instead was combine the quantitative survey method with in-depth interviews and psychological testing. He also used collateral sources of information such as parent and teacher interviews or questionnaires. The result was a contribution to the empirical literature on a critical period of life, a contribution that continues to inform the understanding of people in general and mental health professionals in particular. This empirical approach was used through the subjects' college years and was applied after finding these men over three decades later, in an effort to find out what and who they had become.

The data collected in the 1960's produced findings that were quite surprising to some, off-putting to others. They revealed for one thing that there is, in fact, such a thing as a normal adolescent, one who is not driven by the "Sturm and Drang" ("Storm and Stress") postulated by the theorists of the time. The empirical data described a teenager who is emotionally secure and centered in the mainstream of his parents' culture and values. This teenager was able to cope with the sexual and aggressive "impulses" that the psychoanalytic theory of the time saw as causing rebellion and internal strife. The 1960's and early 1970's data further revealed that, among the normal group, there were three ways of coping, labeled the "three routes," each of which was in the normal range but reflected quite different coping styles of the teens studied.

Various theorists responded by saying in essence that viewing these teenagers as normal was superficial. The data, they said, missed the underlying or repressed turmoil or psychopathology. One theory was that in time the normal-looking teenagers would do worse, expressing later the psychopathology they did not (and should have) expressed in their adolescence. Just wait and see, they warned.

In fact, we did wait and see. In studying these men after the passage of decades, we in effect asked the data to tell us what happens over time to persons who were normal as adolescents. Would their normality persist? Or would it dissolve in the flux and challenges of adult life, leaving any semblance of normality a pale memory next to the reality of present emotional turmoil?

As we shall describe, no ostensible psychopathology was found at any point. A major finding of this book is that the normality of these men, shown over 34 years ago, persists, refuting the insistent theorists of adolescent turmoil and disarray.

The longitudinal data was also used to address whether the three ways of coping within the normal range persisted over the decades. In fact, as we shall show, the groups had largely similar outcomes.

In short, writing this book describes a reunion of sorts, with subjects first studied thirty-four years earlier. A group of normal teenagers had been studied in depth three decades earlier, and we wondered what had become of them.

Chapter 2

The High School Years

Our subjects were born at a time (1946–1949) of great optimism and enthusiasm in the United States. The allies had beaten back German, Japanese, and Italian attempts at world hegemony. The U.S. in particular emerged from WWII transcendent, its economy, homeland, and population relatively intact. Only the U.S. had nuclear weapons. The boys were home again from war, ready to start families and pursue the American dream. Their young brides were quite cooperative. There was a pent-up demand for goods after years of war-related rationing. Highways that had been built to bolster national defense provided pathways to ever expanding suburbs. The young post-WWII couples set right out growing their families, leading to the start of the storied "baby boom," of which our subjects were a part. That demographic surge still makes its influence felt as the U.S. braces for this group to begin retiring en mass in the year 2008.

In 1962, our subjects were 14 years old. They were in high school between 1962 and 1966. The 1960's, of course, were legendary in their own right. It may not be coincidental that youth seemed to loom so large in that era (Abbe Hoffman, famed prankster and member of the "Chicago 7" in the 1960's, denied he was the first one who said one shouldn't trust anyone over the age of 30, but did not disagree with the sentiment). The work of Holinger & Offer (1982) provides evidence that the population density of youth helps shape the consciousness of youth in each generation. Teenagers in the 1960's were like an apotheosis of the spirit that created them in such numbers: vibrant, self-defined, hopeful. A portion of them, perhaps the most vociferous and visible, were "hippies," who glorified in defying convention and declaring the beginning of a new era. As Bob Dylan sang, "Come mothers and fathers throughout the land, don't criticize what you can't understand, get out of the road if you can't lend a hand, for the times are a changing."

While our subjects lived in the 1960's, they were not stereotypical creatures of it. They typically did not smoke pot, engage in promiscuous sex, or join mass protests against the war in Vietnam or for civil rights. Yet they could not have been unaware of these activities, which were so well publicized by the media. Our subjects were centered in a different way, flowing down what has turned out to be the mainstream in America. The hippies and activists seemed to get all the publicity, but eventually almost all of them seemed to cut their hair, give up pot, and return to the place our subjects never left. Our subjects reflected the energy and enthusiasm of the times. But that energy and enthusiasm did not veer toward the rebellious, dramatic, or the extreme. Instead they remained centered on mainstream values and moved in the general direction their parents had.

Our research indicates that they remained centered on a core of values and self-definition. There was a stability, a psychological equilibrium, among these psychologically normal teenagers that acknowledged and reacted to, but was not overwhelmed by, the events that swirled around them.

There appears to be little reason, looking back, to think these students would be filled with turmoil or angst. Primarily they were from middle to upper middle class suburban families, raised in one of the most powerful and prosperous nations in world history. Vietnam was a source of anxiety, but not an imminent personal one for most of these college-bound high school students. People anguished about communism, nuclear weapons, and civil rights. But for most of these students, such matters were abstractions, not impacting or dominating the consciousness of their daily lives.

Nevertheless, the dominant psychiatric and psychological theories of the time did not predict these or any group of mainstream adolescents would be happy, well-adjusted, or positive in their outlook. Teenagers, most psychiatrists and psychologists of that era believed, were at odds with their own impulses. Puberty resurrected sexual conflicts that long ago had been apparently resolved. The thinking of the teenager, these professionals asserted, became rebellious. They were prone to violence and other antisocial behavior. The drive of the teenager was to repudiate parents and all traditions. Mental health experts believed parents could not control adolescents. A cottage industry focusing on treating adolescents in in-patient psychiatric settings emerged. Teachers did not know what to do about difficult teenagers. The police were often used as a last resort in dealing with them.

Webster (1956) defined turmoil as "tumult, disturbance, confusion and uproar." These words do accurately describe the process clinically disturbed adolescents go through during adolescence. But psychiatrists and psychologists assumed that normal, mentally healthy adolescents inevitably have similar experiences. As noted, it has long been their axiom that the study of psychopathology is the best way to understand normal psychology. In the 1960's, the view of adolescents as rent with turmoil and rebellion seemed almost self-evidently true. The tendency was—if one were confronted with a distraught or out-of-control teenager—to shrug and say, "What do you expect?" or "It's just a stage he's going through." If a teenager did not manifest turmoil, he was seen as repressing his impulses or not progressing normally, with possible dire consequences for his future adjustment.

The psychoanalyst, Anna Freud, put it most cogently when she said, "the upholding of a steady equilibrium during the adolescent process is itself abnormal" (A. Freud, 1958). Yet the studies she was relying on primarily had been done on clinically disturbed adolescents and juvenile delinquents. One could ask, what about the vast number of adolescents who simply grew up quietly without stirring up anybody, anywhere?

The main reason that we undertook to study a group of normal, mentally healthy adolescents was to determine how in fact normal teenagers go through adolescence. Are they indeed full of "Sturm and Drang" as they go through high school? Do they oscillate between the various extremes of psychological functioning, being happy and carefree one day and deeply depressed just 24 hours later? Or are they like normal persons in other stages of life—reasonably happy and well-adjusted, subject to varying moods or emotions depending on the circumstances—but not buffeted by extremes of uncontrollable impulses, irrational depression, anxiety, or despair.

When we began our study in the Fall of 1962, our goal was to select a group of mentally healthy freshman boys from two high schools in the Chicago area. We planned to study subjects' adjustment throughout high school, to let the data tell us what normal adolescents really are like. As it turned out, however, initial results were met by a hailstorm of criticism. Many psychiatrists and psychologists took the position that these adolescents' apparent good adjustment was superficial and that during their college years, they would fall apart and their true inner turmoil would become manifest.

So we undertook, with the help of a second government grant, to study them four years after high school, to the end of their college years. Our purpose at that point was to generate another empirical test of the inevitable-turmoil theory of adolescence.

To accomplish our study, we selected adolescent males from two Midwestern high schools during the first month of their freshman year in 1962. They were primarily from middle to upper middle-income families. At that time, there was no psychological test for adolescents that we felt met our needs, i.e. one that could be given to freshman boys to select a group that was relatively mentally healthy.

As a result, we constructed the Offer Self-Image Questionnaire (OSIQ) for adolescents (Offer, et al. 1969 and 1992) using information available to us in 1960 and 1961 on what areas were important to the adolescent. The questionnaire had 129 items and twelve scales (see Appendix B). The OSIQ assesses teenagers' adjustment in areas such as impulse control, emotional well-being, peer relationships, family relationships, coping ability, and sexuality.

Originally, the questionnaire was constructed for the sole purpose of helping us select our research sample. Over the years, however, the OSIQ became a popular psychological test used in many countries throughout the world. At Northwestern University Medical School in Chicago, Illinois, we have a bank of data provided by 30,000 adolescents both normal and psychiatrically disturbed or delinquent. Data are available as well with respect to adolescents with specific medical problems such as cystic fibrosis, leukemia, diabetes, or kidney disease. It has been used in English speaking countries and also has been translated into twenty-six languages including: Spanish, Chinese, French, Dutch, Slovenian, Swiss-French, Japanese, Turkish, Czeck, Hungarian, Finnish, German, Italian, Bengali, Arabic, Hebrew, Hindu-Indian, Polish, Indonesian, Korean, Malaysian, and Portuguese. Over the course of 40 years, the OSIQ has become a widely used resource shedding light internationally on adolescent functioning.

Using the OSIQ, subjects were selected whose self-image was within one standard deviation of the mean on at least nine out of twelve scales. In other words, these subjects described themselves as within the statistically average range with respect to the majority of areas important to adolescent functioning. The boys had at least a C average during eighth grade and were not under psychiatric care. The parents of each confirmed their son was mentally healthy.

School records were available to the researchers; and the homeroom teacher completed two sets of ratings on the boys, one during their freshman year and one during their junior year. Each subject was interviewed twice yearly during the high school years. In addition, a battery of psychological tests was administered at age sixteen. The interviews covered the psychological world of the teenager. How did they cope with high school? How did they get along with their parents, siblings, friends, and teachers? Did they have any psychiatric symptoms? If so, what and how severe were they? Did they engage in anti-social or delinquent behavior? Did they take any drugs? What about their sexuality?

Originally we had 84 subjects. Seven subjects moved away by the time our interviews started in the spring of 1963. The father of one of the subjects did not allow his son to participate; and two subjects refused even though their parents encouraged them to participate. One subject's mother died a few weeks before his scheduled interview, and he refused to participate even though his father encouraged him to do so. Accordingly, when we began our interviews, we had 73 subjects.

These are the major findings from the high school part of the study (see Offer, 1969).

1. The vast majority of our subjects did not show any extremes of mood. Their relationships with parents, siblings, and peers were on the whole quite good. Some were excellent students, others just average; but no one was failing. Most were active in sports, had an active social life, and

had lots of after-school activities (chess club, debating societies, scouts, music lessons, or extra-mural sports).

2. Of the 73 subjects, only seven exhibited clinical symptoms to even a minor degree. The seven who did experience clinical symptoms showed an appreciable degree of adolescent turmoil. The rest of our subjects, 90 percent, experienced only minor turmoil during their high school years. This was true both at home and at school. In the vast majority, there was no progression to psychological disequilibrium and tumult, or marked fluctuant and unpredictable behavior. Emotional and behavioral indices gained through interviews of the adolescents and their parents, teacher ratings, and analysis of psychological testing, all negated the existence of turmoil on a massive scale in our adolescent subjects. Most of the conflicts between them and their parents took place in junior high school (7th and 8th grade). Both parents and teens were able to cope with that conflict before it grew to chaotic proportions for the individuals involved. The adolescent tumult one might expect from reading the professional and lay literature in the 1960's simply was not seen in the vast majority of our subjects.

3. Our data showed that rebellion is part of the quest of teenagers to emancipate from their parents. In our subjects, however, rebellion was fought over issues that seem to an outsider small and undramatic. Bickering best characterizes these fights. The teenager's parents, for instance, wanted him to turn the radio off and study; his response was to keep the radio on and claim he could not study without it. If they wanted him to buy new clothes, the old ones were good enough. If they told him he could not buy new clothes, new ones were essential. The adolescent tends to define what he does in terms of what his parents do not want him to do. But, importantly, this rebellion was not predictive of rejection of the essence of their parental values.

4. If we define delinquency as engaging in acts that could result in having a police record, our subjects were not delinquent. As noted, that does not mean that they were free of rebellious behavior. But most of their "anti" behavior was directed towards their parents. Rarely was it directed towards the schools or the community in which they lived. It involved issues such as taking out the garbage, how to dress, when to come home, whether to make their beds, and who their friends should be. The teens were very aware of having to curb their impulses. By the time the adolescents entered high school, fights and disagreements with parents were reduced dramatically. Some of the adolescents we studied did engage in delinquent activities, such as stealing money or food from stores, overturning garbage cans after an exciting football game, vandalism, physical fights, and on rare occasion, stealing cars. Most of our subjects, however, committed only one delinquent act and then abandoned this form of

behavior. Only three percent of our sample had chronic difficulties in controlling their impulses. Two received psychotherapy. The third should have but did not.

5. The normal adolescent, we found, accepted his parents' basic values. The relationship between the adolescent and his parents was based on the teen's acceptance of living in a particular culture and of its norms. The fact is that most adolescents followed in the footsteps of their parents. Is that a new discovery? We do not think so. In the 1960's, for instance, the vast majority of adolescent participants in civil rights marches came from liberal homes where their actions were fully approved.

6. Our data clearly showed that, for the vast majority of the subjects, there was no major gap of understanding and communication between the generations. What we learned is that members of mentally healthy families understood what society expects of them, and tried to live up to this expectation. When normal adolescents did not do so, they were acutely aware they are departing from their parents' values. Minor rebellions helped the teenager to separate from his parents and become an independent person. The person he was, however, tended—much more than the teenager could realize at the time—to replicate the social/psychological world of his parents. Teens and their parents had a basic understanding of what is important. They shared the same basic values. These values include religious, moral, ethical, and political standards of the individual. They also encompassed the individual's goals and aspirations in life as well as attitudes towards education, work, and social/familial relations. Not included were preferences in music, clothes, food, or videos.

7. The normal teenage boy, we found, wanted to grow up and be very much like his father. His relationship with his father typically was rather emotionally distant. He admired his father, however, and consulted him on issues that dealt with their vocational and educational interests. His mother was his emotional anchor. Emotional issues were discussed with her. If he had problems in the social sphere, in school, or in sports, his mother was the one who would listen to her son and advise him about what to do. The normal teenager saw his mother as warm and understanding, and although he was, at times, ambivalent towards her, he felt that they understand one another. The only area that was never discussed with either parent was sexuality. The normal teen received information on this important area from his peers or his own personal experiences. In general, we learned, the emotional security of each generation is vital in maintaining and developing bridges from both sides.

8. The adolescents, we learned, liked the community in which they grew up. In the future, they wanted to live in a community similar to the one they

lived in now. They felt sorry for anyone not living in an "open, beautiful community" like theirs. These adolescents, we believe, were representative of a large number of adolescents living in suburban America. They were less visible or prominent in the discourse of adults than other teenagers might be because they were, in a sense, less noisy. They shared the values of their parents and society; were able to communicate effectively with adults; and have fewer problems and move into adulthood with relative ease and comfort.

9. There was nothing as conflictual to the adolescent we studied in the early 1960's as was his sexuality. The students received very little sexual education during adolescence. There were no formal courses in high school or in religious (Sunday) school. Their parents rarely, if ever, talked to their sons about sexuality. So the young man was left to find out for himself. It was the one area that the subjects often asked us what we found to be "the norm." Despite this difficulty, most of the subjects, learned to discover his true feelings in the area of sexuality, to successfully navigate through the maze of adult double sexual standards and hypocrisy, as well as explicit and implicit peer opinions in this area.

10. Almost all of our subjects had reached puberty by their freshman year. However, talking to the subjects about their sexual experiences was difficult. They would not answer directly, get embarrassed, or refuse to answer questions altogether. By their junior year, thirty percent had told us that they had experienced heavy petting. Ten percent had had sexual intercourse. Not one reported having had a homosexual experience. Almost all of our subjects daydreamed about girls, movie stars, rock singers, or new young teachers. Only a minority (about 25 percent) daydreamed about a girl they knew. All our subjects thought that their mother was attractive, which was not always corroborated, at least in our opinion, by our interviews of the mothers.

11. By the end of the freshman year, in high school, we found, only forty-five percent of the boys had been on a date. The ones who did not, did not feel abnormal about not having done so. It was often the parents, and especially the mothers, who wanted their sons to date. As they got older, things changed. By their senior year, ninety-five percent of our subjects were dating. The five percent who did not, were extremely shy and felt abnormal about it.

12. During the high school years, 10 of our 73 subjects experienced at least one major crisis. Four had lost their fathers; three experienced their parents going through divorce; two had life-threatening injuries; and one saw his brother become crippled for life. On the whole, our subjects were able to cope with these difficult situations well. They were able to

make the best of the situation. In other words, they were resilient and showed great inner strength.

To summarize the high school years of our subjects, it is stability and not turmoil that was the overriding characteristic of our subjects. The major question from a developmental point of view was what would happen to our subjects when they changed their milieu and left home to go to college, work, or the Army. Would their stability continue?

Chapter 3

The Young Adulthood Years

INITIAL FINDINGS

After the high school data collection phase ended, subjects were followed yearly for four years (1967–1971) (Offer and Offer, 1975) through interviews and psychological testing. Parents filled out forms describing their children's adjustment. Analyses based on these data combined with data collected during the subjects' high school years, are described in this chapter.

After high school, 80 percent of our subjects went to college; 12 percent joined the Armed Forces; and eight percent went directly to work. Sixty-one of the original 73 subjects (or 84 percent) were studied in the four-year post-high-school study. (The reader may note that a smaller percentage participated in the 4-year follow-up than they did in the 34-year follow-up. This reflects the great effort put into the 34-year study and the difference is not an error.) During the first post-high-school year, parents were asked to rate the adjustment and behavior of their sons via mail. The subjects were asked via mail to complete the Hess and Henry Identity Scale (Hess, Henry and Sims, 1968) (see Appendix C). During the second post-high-school year, all 61 subjects were interviewed in person in Dr. Offer's office at Michael Reese Hospital in Chicago. During the third post-high-school year, they were again interviewed in person. During the fourth post-high-school year, the subjects were asked to respond to a self-rating scale about their adjustment via mail.

Of the 80 percent (49 individuals) who went to college, 10 went to various junior colleges in the Chicago metropolitan area; 14 went to various branches of the University of Illinois; and the remaining 21 went to these colleges and universities:

Beloit College   University of California—L.A.
Brandeis University   University of Chicago
Carleton College   University of Colorado
Knox College   University of Florida
Oklahoma State University   University of Indiana
Purdue University   University of Iowa
Stanford University   University of Michigan
Vanderbilt University   University of Mississippi
Washington and Jefferson College   University of Missouri
Washington University—St. Louis   University of New Mexico

Obviously, subjects expressed their individuality with respect to which college they were going to go to. Aside from the University of Illinois and Chicago junior colleges, only one college was chosen by more than one subject.

In the analysis of the data from the four high school years and four post-high-school years, we selected 55 variables that had sufficient variability and that separated the group into meaningful subgroups. Using tests of association, we found various relationships between healthy adaptation at the end of the fourth post-high-school year and six psychosocial factors that were collected from six to eight years earlier. (All are significant beyond the .05 level.)

1. The higher the academic standing of the student in the first year of high school, the healthier he appeared to the psychiatrist at the end of college, the slower he was to become involved with the opposite sex, and the more academically successful he was in college.
2. The higher the socioeconomic class of the father, the more positive the son's feelings toward education were at the end of college and the better the relationship between father and son was.
3. The better the teacher's ratings of the emotional and social states of their students in the beginning of high school, the healthier the subject appeared to the psychiatrist at the end of college, and the more successful the subject was in progressing toward the goals he has set for himself.
4. Two percent of our subjects were black and one percent was Hispanic. The less prejudiced the subject was toward blacks, the better student he was academically, the better his home environment, the more positive his attitude toward work, and the higher the mental health ratings by the psychiatrist.
5. The more anxiety and depression the subject displayed, the less likable he appears to the rater. The more depression that was manifested, the poorer his relationship with the interviewer and the greater his need for psychiatric treatment. The more depressed the student appeared in high

school, the more likely it was that he needed psychotherapy after high school. The more the parents approved of the goals their son had set for himself, the less need existed for psychiatric treatment.

It should be noted that these findings were obtained despite the "restrictions of range" presented by our subjects' overall good functioning. It would be expected that relationships would be even stronger in a more diverse sample.

From these findings, we can see meaningful combinations between certain social and environmental factors, such as high school achievement and dating patterns, and psychological indices of health. The psychological measures were determined both by the perception of others and the subjects' self-evaluations.

TYPAL ANALYSES

The next step was to factor analyze the 55 variables. We obtained 10 factors. Thereafter, a typal-analysis was done in order to separate the sample into meaningful subgroups (see Offer and Offer, 1975, for details of this method). Various normal growth patterns were obtained. We gave them the following names: 1) continuous growth; 2) surgent growth; and 3) tumultuous growth. Below we will describe the main psychological characteristics of these three growth patterns.

Continuous Growth

The subjects described within the continuous-growth grouping, 23% progressed throughout adolescence with a smoothness of purpose and self-assurance of their progression toward a meaningful and fulfilling adult life. They were favored by circumstances and mastered previous developmental stages without serious setbacks. Their genetic and environmental backgrounds were excellent.

The family lives had not involved extremely stressful and upsetting events. Their childhoods had been unmarked by death or serious illnesses of a parent or sibling. The nuclear family remained a stable unit throughout childhood and adolescence. The subjects accepted the general cultural and societal norms and felt comfortable within that context. They had the capacity to integrate experiences and to use them as a stimulus for growth.

The parents of these subjects were able to encourage their children's independence. The parents themselves grew and changed with their children. Throughout the eight years of the study, there was basic mutual respect, trust, and affection between the generations. The ability to allow the sons' independence in many areas was undoubtedly facilitated by the sons' behavior patterns. Since the boys were not behaving in a manner clearly divergent from that of the parents, the parents could continue to be provided with need-gratification through their sons. The sense of gratification was reciprocal, with the sons' gaining both from the parents' good feelings toward them and from the parental willingness to allow them to create their own individual lives outside of the household. The value systems of the subjects in this group dovetailed with those of their parents. In many ways the subjects were functioning as continuations of the parents, living not so much the lives the parents had wished for but not attained but, rather, lives similar to those of the parents.

During the high school years, the parent of the opposite sex was the one who was most important for the healthy development of the adolescent. Through her, the teenager tested his sexuality, identity, and potential worth as an adult.

These subjects showed a capacity for good interpersonal relationships. They had close male friends in whom they could confide. Their relationships with the opposite sex became increasingly important as they reached the end of their high school years. Intimacy in the Eriksonian sense (Erikson, 1950) was being developed and was a goal toward which they were striving. Not until they graduated from high school, however, did they begin to develop meaningful relationships with members of the opposite sex.

Subjects described by the continuous-growth pattern acted in accordance with their consciences. There was little evidence of superego problems. Instead they developed meaningful ego ideals, often identifying with persons they knew and admired within the family or at school. The subjects were able to identify feelings of shame and guilt. They proceeded to explain not only how the experiences provoking those responses had affected them but also how they brought closure to the uncomfortable situations. They frequently described a subsequent similar experience, but one that they had been prepared to handle better, putting the earlier upsetting experience into a past time frame of immaturity conquered.

The fantasy lives of the subjects in the continuous group were proactive. They were almost always able to translate their fantasies into reality and action. They could dream about being the best in the class academically, sexually, or athletically. But their actions were guided by a pragmatic and realistic appraisal of their own abilities and of external circumstances. Thus, they avoided confronting repeated disappointments. As an example of their solid reality testing, 85 percent of the subjects got into the colleges of their first choice; they simply did not apply to colleges they could not get into.

Adolescents in the continuous group could postpone immediate gratification and work in a sustained manner toward a future goal. Their delay mechanisms worked well. They tended to temporarily suppress, rather than repress, affect. Generally, they were successful in responding to their aggressive and sexual impulses without being overwhelmed and without acting out in a self-destructive manner. They did not experience prolonged periods of anxiety or depression, two of the most frequent affects described by the entire subject population, including this subgroup. When confronted by external trauma, these subjects usually were able to cope by adaptive action. When difficulties arose, they used the defenses of denial and isolation to protect their egos from being bombarded with affect.

At the end of their fourth post-high-school year, none of the adolescents had received psychotherapy or were thought by the researchers to need psychiatric treatment. There were no psychotic, schizophrenic, borderline, or delinquent adolescents among them. They had no psychosomatic illness and were, in general, in excellent physical health.

Members of the continuous-growth group shared many of the qualities that appear when mental health is viewed in an ideal sense. No single subject ever portrayed all those qualities, and each usually had some difficulty in one or another area. What was most distinctive about members of the continuous-growth group was their overall contentment with themselves and their place in life. Persons in this group were happier than persons in the other two groups. They generally had an order to their lives that could suffer setbacks but that would not yield to psychological symptoms or chaotic behavior as they progressed through the adolescent and young adult years and matured cognitively and emotionally.

Surgent Growth

The surgent-growth group (35%), although functioning as adaptively as the first group, was characterized by important enough differences in ego structure, background, and family environment to constitute a different subgroup. Developmental spurts are illustrative of the growth pattern of the surgent-growth group.

One of the major differences between the surgent-growth subjects and those in the continuous-growth group was their genetic and environmental backgrounds. The background of the surgent-growth adolescents was not as free of problems and traumas as that of their continuous-growth peers. The nuclear families in the surgent-growth group were more likely to have been affected by separation, death, or severe illnesses.

For the subjects described in the surgent-growth category, relationships with parents were marked by some minor conflicts of opinions and values. There were areas of disagreement between father and mother concerning basic issues, such as the importance of discipline, academic attainments, and religious beliefs. In several cases the parents came from different backgrounds. The mothers of some of these adolescents had difficulty in letting their children grow and in separating from them.

These subjects were not as confident as were the boys in the continuous-growth group; their self-esteem wavered. They relied on positive reinforcement derived from the opinions of important others, such as parents and peers. When that reinforcement was not forthcoming, they often became discouraged about themselves and their abilities. As a group, they were able to form meaningful interpersonal relationships similar to those of the subjects in the continuous-growth group, but the relationships were maintained with a greater degree of effort.

Some subjects differed from the continuous-growth group in the amount of emotional conflict they experienced and in their patterns of resolving conflicts. More concentrated energy appeared to be required to master developmental tasks than was true for members of the continuous-growth group. At times, these subjects adjusted very well, integrating their experiences and moving ahead; at other times, they seemed to be stuck at a premature closure and unable to move forward. A cycle of progression and regression was more typical of this group than of the continuous-growth group. The defenses they used, anger and projection, represent more psychopathology than do the defenses used by the first group.

Although subjects in this category were able to cope successfully with their average expectable environment (Hartmann, 1958), their ego development was not adequate for coping with unanticipated sources of anxiety. Affects that were usually flexible and available would, at times of crisis, such as the death of a close relative, become stringently controlled and less available. That, together with their being not as action oriented as the first group, made them slightly more prone to depression. The depression would accompany or openly follow the highly controlled affect. On other occasions, when their defense mechanisms faltered, they experienced moderate anxiety and a short period of turmoil resulted. When disappointed in themselves or others, they showed a tendency to use projection and anger.

The subjects worked toward their vocational goals sporadically or with a lack of enthusiasm, but they were able to keep their long-range behavior in line with their general expectations for themselves.

The group as a whole was less introspective than either the first or the third group. The over all adjustment of these subjects, however, was often just as adaptive and successful as that of the first group. But the adjustment was achieved with less self-examination and a more controlled drive or surge toward development. Suppression of emotionality was characteristic of the subjects in the surgent-growth group. A small number of this group needed and received counseling or psychotherapy. The psychotherapy was for transient problems. No chronic emotional problems emerged in this group.

Tumultous Growth

The third group, the tumultuous-growth group, had traits in some ways similar to the problematic adolescents often described in psychiatric, psychoanalytic, and social science literature. Nevertheless, they functioned well enough as to be considered psychologically in the normal range. These were students who go through adolescence with much internal turmoil, which manifests itself in limited overt behavioral problems in school and in the home.

The subjects demonstrating tumultuous-growth patterns came from less stable backgrounds than did the subjects in the other two groups. Some of the parents of this group had overt marital conflicts, and others had a history of mental illness in the family. Hence, the genetic and environmental backgrounds of the subjects in the tumultuous-growth group were decidedly different from those of the other two groups. Also present was a social class difference. The study population was primarily middle-class, but this group contained many subjects who belonged to the lower middle-class. For them, functioning in a largely middle-class and upper middle-class environment may have been a cause for additional stress.

Strong family bonds were present within the tumultuous-growth group, as they were within each of the other patterns. Separation from their sons was more painful for the parents of the tumultuous-growth group, however, and it became a source of continuing conflict for the subjects. The parent-son relationships characterizing this group were similar to those of many of the neurotic patients seen in outpatient psychotherapy. Further, parent-son communication of a system of values was poorly defined or contradictory.

Subjects in the tumultuous group were considerably more dependent on peer culture than were their age mates in the other groups, possibly because they received fewer gratifications from relationships within the family. When they experienced a personal loss, such as the ending of a relationship with a good friend, their depression was deeper than that of persons from the other two groups, although only very rarely associated with suicidal feelings and impulses.

The tumultuous-growth group began dating at a younger age than did their peers in the other two groups. For these early adolescent boys, a relationship with a girl was one of dependency, with the girl being a substitute for a mothering figure. In late adolescence, for some, however, their heterosexual relationships gained meaning, and they were able to appreciate the personal characteristics of their female friends.

Many subjects in the tumultuous-growth group were highly sensitive and introspective. They were usually aware of their emotional needs. Academically, overall they were less interested in science, engineering, law, and medicine than in the arts, the humanities, and the social and psychological sciences. However, business and engineering careers remained the usual choices for this group, as well as for the first two groups.

These subjects were observed to have recurrent self-doubts while at the same time engaging in braggadocio. They manifested escalating conflicts with their parents, and debilitating inhibitions. They often responded inconsistently to their social and academic environments. The self-doubts of the tumultuous subjects continued throughout the high school and college years. These doubts represented internal difficulty at integrating internal experience with the expectations placed on them by the outside world.

The ability of this group to appreciate and probe reality and act accordingly was relatively strong, in contrast to patient populations. But disappointment in others and in themselves when contrasted to the other groups was prevalent. Action was accompanied by more anxiety and depression in this group than in the other two groups. Emotional turmoil was an integral part of their separation and individuation process. Without the tumult, growth toward independence and meaningful interpersonal relationships was questionable. Wide mood swings indicated a search for who they were as separate persons and a concern about whether their activities were worthwhile. Feelings of mistrust of the adult world were often expressed in this group. Affect was readily available and created both intensely pleasurable and intensely painful experiences. Changes in self-concept could precipitate moderately severe anxiety reactions. Only slowly, and with the help of a long psychosocial moratorium, were adjustment problems eventually overcome.

As a group, these subjects did not do as well academically during their high school years as did subjects from the first two groups. Over the eight years, however, they did just as well as those in the other two groups. As with other variables, academic success differentiated the groups, but honor students and average students could be found within each group.

These subjects needed and used more energy than usual to cope with the everyday problems that a subject has to deal with. If everything went relatively well, they felt good. When unexpected disappointment came their way, they had a hard time dealing with it. It took them longer and they used more psychic energy than subjects in the other two groups to get over the disappointment.

The tumultuous-growth group members experienced more events as major psychological traumas than did members of the other groups. The difficulties in their life situations were greater than the satisfactions. Defenses were not well developed for handling emotionally trying situations. A relatively high percentage of this group had overt clinical problems and had received psychotherapy. The subjects in this group experienced more psychological pain than did the others.

FURTHER FINDINGS

There was a mixed group of students (21%), whose scores did not fall within any of the previously described three groups. This group comprised about 20 percent of the total. Their profiles were a mixture of the three groups.

The revealed differences technique, comparing teenagers' and their parents' responses to parallel questionnaire items, was used for evaluating the strength and the openness of family communication. That method clearly differentiated the families along the three developmental routes. The best understanding between the generations was observed among the continuous-growth group, and the least understanding was observed in the tumultuous-growth group, with the surgent-group in between (Offer et al., 1975).

In short, these data (Offer and Offer, 1975) showed three fundamental, normal routes through adolescence and young adulthood. The first group of our sample progressed continuously and developed values similar to those of their parents. A second group developed in spurts with periodic turmoil. The third group experienced the years from 14 to 21 with some of the turmoil frequently held to characterize all adolescents; for them, the developmental tasks leading to normal development were difficult but ultimately attainable.

What we didn't know is how the subjects we studied would progress through adulthood, in this case, into middle age. Gaining that knowledge was the goal toward which the follow-up study that underlies this book was dedicated.

Tony, Bob, Carl: Adolescence and Young Adulthood
Examples of Continuous, Surgent, and Tumultuous Adaptation

In the first phase of the study, Offer and Offer (1975) selected three boys as exemplars of the three types of normal adaptation during adolescence, continuous, surgent, and tumultuous. All three subjects participated in the 1990's follow-up study. Their stories are presented in this book. First, we will focus on their lives beginning in their teenage years through young adulthood. Then, in a separate chapter, we will describe their lives thereafter, through age 48.

TONY

In 1975, Tony was selected to represent the Continuous Growth group. This group was characterized by positive adjustment to both internal and external demands. The teenagers in this group comfortably accepted general cultural and societal norms. They could integrate their experiences and use them as a stimulus for growth. Consistent with teenagers in this group, the 1975 data about Tony reflected self-confidence, positive outlook, and good relationships with parents and siblings. He was popular and academically successful in high school and college. His approach was practical and adaptive. To quote from Offer and Offer (1975), "Basically, he exhibited a contentment with himself as a successful and happy human being." Tony's story through college follows.

Most people remember high school as a difficult and confusing time in their lives, if not downright miserable. Not Tony Canfield. Although he was somewhat short and stocky until his junior year, with fair skin prone to breakouts, his regular, all-American features and self-confident manner conveyed the impression of above-average looks. He was also an excellent athlete, considered one of the top players on the school hockey team, as well as an academic achiever, with honor roll caliber grades. Years later, Tony looked back on his adolescent years as a time of contentment. "I liked sports and I got along fine in academics, I had a girlfriend," he said, "I think it was a pretty happy time."

Tony was generally contented with his home life as well. "We always felt loved," he observed. He was raised in a middle class home in the suburbs of Chicago, the second of three children. Tony and his elder brother, Jim, were born just 16 months apart; his sister, Carol, was eight years younger. Tony's father, Dan, worked as a repairman in a mid-sized electronics firm, and his mother, Joanne, was a housewife. The Canfields belonged to a Presbyterian church and attended regularly, though as an adult, Tony did not recall religion playing much of a role in his upbringing: "We probably went during Christmas, Easter, that sort of thing," he remarked. Dan and Joanne, who had begun dating when they were in high school, were both from stable families as well; Dan was an only child, but Joanne had been close to her sisters when she was growing up and remained so throughout her adult life.

The one area of struggle in Tony's home life was the degree of discipline exerted by his parents. As a rule, the Canfields kept a close eye on Tony and his siblings. "If I know who my children are with and where they are, I can relax more," said his father, jokingly adding: "I am known as 'Scrooge' because I am a stickler on the curfew." In general, Tony's mother, Joanne, was responsible for enforcing house rules, and Tony believed Joanne's sternness occasionally bordered on authoritarian. "Mom sometimes would be very strict and it was unfair," he said. "With my father, I knew I had done something bad and I deserved it, but sometimes the discipline I received from mom was upsetting and confusing." But even when Tony chafed at his mother's strictness, the foundation of his strong emotional connection with her was unshaken. "My mother was an unselfish person who would give up anything for us," he recalled as an adult.

While Tony's father, Dan, sought to keep a tight grip on his children, his strictness was tempered by his desire to keep emotional conflicts at bay. Instead, when Tony and his brother argued with their mother during high school, their father often played the role of mediator. "We argue things out," said Dan, "I feel the boys can express their opinions and respect mine." Certainly, Tony greatly preferred his father's disciplinary style to his mother's. "My father's worst trait was to sometimes allow my mother to dictate policy that I felt he should have been involved in and dictated," he commented as an adult. He recalled his father, on the other hand, as someone who "didn't like conflicts," as a general rule. "Dad was an arbitrator and a peacemaker," Tony said. "You could always talk to him about anything."

By the time he was an adolescent, Tony, like his father, had developed an intense distaste for emotional conflict. Although his arguments with his parents were generally over small issues—such as whether he would study or play hockey after school—he inevitably found them upsetting. "My mother gets too excited," he said, "When she gets mad, it is a mad gallery." In his mother's view, their disagreements were insignificant; to the contrary, she found Tony to be reasonable and deferential. "Tony is obedient—we have no discipline problems," she observed, "He likes it peaceful. He gets frustrated if we argue in front of him—he would rather not hear it."

As a high school student, the most important person in Tony's life was undoubtedly his older brother Jim. In addition to being close in age, the siblings looked and talked somewhat alike; they shared a common interest in sports, and both were popular with their peers. "If I had to pick someone to be with on a desert island, it would be my brother," Tony said. Even their father was surprised by how close they were: "If I reprimand one, I have the other to contend with," he said. The relationship between Tony and his sister Carol was very different; when he was in high school, she was still a young girl, and she was rarely included in his day-to-day activities.

Both the Canfield parents were conscious of the importance of not playing favorites among the siblings. "I never sensed that either parent favored any of the three of us," Tony said later. The brothers maintained an unusually non-competitive relationship. "If we were playing sports we would compete but not against each other," said Tony. "Jim was a better student, I was better in sports. When he got good grades, I congratulated him. When I took the SAT the year after him and scored higher, I didn't feel resentment."

Tony's ambitious career plans began early. When he was eight years old, he was in a car accident that caused him to miss much of third grade. The Canfields successfully sued the driver of the car, and Tony spent a good deal of time with the lawyer who represented the family. From then on, he "talked and slept law," said his mother. Tony's passion for his chosen profession encouraged him to push himself hard to maintain a top grade average, deriding teenage vices like smoking and drinking as "crazy." His brother Jim decided early on that he would pursue a law career as well. "This is the influence of Tony's interest," said his father, "He is obsessed with it."

As is common for parents of the adolescents who follow a continuous growth pattern, the Canfields were entirely supportive of their children's career goals, using them to achieve the ambitions they had for themselves but were not able to attain. "I want them to have the things I never had," said Tony's father, Dan, "I had high ambitions—I also wanted to be a lawyer. But the little nudge—the encouragement that you need—just wasn't there. His mother, Joanne, agreed. "I give my children more encouragement than I got," she said.

Tony was intensely—even excessively—driven to excel scholastically. As an adolescent, he described receiving a lower-than-expected grade—a "B" rather than an "A"—and feeling depressed about it. His father, however, provided a source of support: "My father said not to worry about it and so I stopped worrying," he said. By high school, Tony's expectations for himself had even exceeded his parents'. "I think that Tony and his older brother have achieved for themselves, not for me," commented his father.

Both Tony and his brother were considered members of the popular crowds of their grade in high school, nearly always surrounded by a large group of friends. "Tony never wants to be alone," commented his mother. Tony began dating regularly at age fifteen, and never had a problem getting dates: "The most difficult thing about dating is choosing the girl," he joked. In any case, Tony's interest in girls was secondary to his academic ambitions, and he deliberately sought to maintain an emotional—as well as physical—distance from them while dating. His strategy to avoid the "temptation" of sex was to stick to double-dating with another couple, often his brother. "If you have sex during high school, you can get into trouble and have a bad reputation," he noted.

For Tony, maintaining a good "reputation" among his peers was extremely important. Fortunately, by high school he had developed nimble coping skills, as is typical of those following a continuous growth pattern. Often, he was able to alleviate his concerns about how he was viewed by his peers by seeking the approval of his parents or peers, after which he was able to put any bad feelings to rest. "One can reason with emotion," he claimed. Tony recalled an incident where he forgot his lines during a high school drama show and felt ashamed about it. Initially, he had the urge to hide; "I didn't want to see anyone afterwards," he remarked. But instead, he decided to seek reassurance from his fellow drama club members, and as a result, no longer felt that he had terribly embarrassed himself: "My friends told me this happens to other people, so I didn't feel too bad about it," he said.

For most of high school, Tony felt it was unimportant to have a steady girlfriend, instead choosing to casually date many different girls. "It seems to be that way, one year one girl, the next year another one," said his mother. In his final year of high school, Tony did settle on a steady girlfriend, Ann, who had been a childhood friend. He relished Ann's maternal qualities, describing her as "very domestic." In the spring of that year, Tony was accepted at the same Midwestern liberal arts college his brother was already attending, which meant he would be moving several hundred miles away from Ann that fall. Though their relationship had been moving along smoothly, Tony and Ann decided that it made sense to break up at the end of the summer. Tony, while sad about the loss of his relationship, did not allow himself to second-guess his decision based on emotion. "I guess it was for the best, considering the schooling I had to do," he remarked practically.

Unlike other college students, Tony had few financial worries, having been awarded a scholarship, which covered most of his tuition. With his parents footing the bill for the remainder of his expenses, he immediately dove into a full course load of pre-law classes. Obtaining good grades remained a high priority for him, and he kept up a B+/A- average. He was driven even harder by the knowledge that his parents were contributing to his education. "I felt when I was in college that I had to work really hard to please my dad because he was working so hard with both my brother and I in college at the same time, and my sister still at home," he said.

Although Tony and Jim, also a pre-law major, continued to have overlapping social lives in college, Tony felt keenly that they were not as close as they had been in high school. "My relationship with my brother is different now," he said. "Now that we have different roommates, it is a little more difficult." With his grinding class schedule, Tony had less time to devote to his social life, so the loss of his brother's attention became even more significant.

Although he spent little time with male friends in college, Tony did keep up a regular romantic life. He continued to meet and date women with the same ease he had in high school, and persisted in the same pattern of starting and ending relationships after short periods of time. He also continued to view sex as a potential obstacle to career success, and initially refused to bow to the pressure to have a sexual relationship. "The reason I don't have sex has nothing to do with morals," he said, "I am afraid if a girl got pregnant, I would have to leave school and it would ruin my career."

During his sophomore year of college, Tony dated a fellow student, Amy, steadily for the entire year. At this point, he began to feel torn between his sexual desires and his belief that sex would interfere with his ambitions. "Should I feel my wild oats or shouldn't I?" he asked, "Should I try to make it with girls, or just settle down with the girl I like now?" Though the prospect of marriage appealed to him, he again worried that it could affect career aspirations. "Is there a statistical correlation between marriage and success in school?" he wondered. This time, Tony did not let his desire for sexual experience stand in the way of pragmatism. "The problem is, I will have to study for so many years and I can't support myself and a wife," he explained.

Tony's parents also continued to wield a great deal of influence over him in college. Although he felt that his political views had become "a little more liberal" than his parents, he remained tied to them, financially and emotionally, throughout most of college. Once again, he expressed a certain amount of irritation with his mother, noting that she still treated him "like a high school student." Yet when he considered marriage to Amy, he turned to his parents for advice. "I might marry her if my parents don't object, but if they have anything [negative] to say about it, I will not," he said. As Tony suspected, his parents discouraged the marriage. "I think Tony should not get married until the end of college, or until he starts law school," said his mother.

During his senior year of college, Tony met Rhonda, who seemed like the perfect companion for his single-minded ambitions. "There was a physical attraction and she was a very independent person," he said, "Rhonda is more of an extrovert, not shy, vivacious, and yet in a certain way conservative in her actions," he said. After so many years of devoting himself to academics, Tony realized that his social life had suffered terribly. With her bubbly personality, Rhonda neatly solved that problem for him. "She is very outgoing and makes friends easily which I have a bit of a problem with, so she is a great social buffer," he admitted. The relationship quickly became serious. "We spent a lot of time together, seeing each other almost every day," he said.

After dating Rhonda for several months, Tony decided that, for the first time, he wanted to prioritize a relationship over his career ambitions. "My mother said, you are getting too serious, you should break up with this girl," he said. He ignored his mother's advice and continued to date Rhonda. He also appreciated Rhonda's willingness to be a supporting player in his perpetually demanding lifestyle, which he had no intention of changing. "Rhonda is very caring and nurturing," he said. Within a year of meeting her, Tony had determined that he wanted to marry Rhonda, though he did not feel financially secure enough to do so immediately.

Just before he graduated from college, Tony was accepted to a rigorous seven-year combined J.D./Ph.D. program in forensic psychology, confirming his belief that he had the capabilities to achieve his far-reaching ambitions. His relationship with Rhonda continued to progress, and the two moved to Chicago and found an apartment together so Tony could start his graduate studies. Altogether, Tony was pleased to be continuing on the path he had shaped for himself at a very young age: "No outstanding events have happened to me," he said, "I have changed very little." It was true: with an extremely bright career future and a devoted companion by his side, at age 22, Tony appeared to be sailing on the same smooth waters he had throughout his adolescent years.

From high school through college, Tony exemplifies the Continuous adaptation to adolescence and then young adulthood. Tony at this point in his life is unashamedly and unequivocally in the mainstream of his parents' values and aspirations. His family background is solid and supportive. There is clear reciprocal admiration and gratification between parents and son. Tony excelled in high school, not just academically but interpersonally. But he didn't let his success overwhelm him. He was able to cope with setbacks successfully, without turmoil. He lived values he had internalized and felt good about it. There was a smooth interchange between values and self-esteem. His goals for himself were realistic and then eventually realized reinforcing his sense of competence. His course had continued in an almost unwavering way through college and presumable would do so into his post-graduate studies.

BOB

Offer and Offer (1975) described the Surgent Growth group as characterized by fluctuations in the quality of their adjustment. At times, they adjusted well. At other times, they seemed to stall, experiencing periods of anger or placing blame upon others. They tended to react to crises with over control. When overwhelmed, they tended to become anxious or somewhat depressed. Their self esteem was more fragile than that of boys in the Continuous Growth group.

In the 1975 book, Bob was selected as an exemplar of this group. As is characteristic of this group, Bob did not follow a smooth path through adolescence. But he functioned well within the normal range. His story through his college years follows.

As a freshman in high school, Bob Rubin did not stand out of the crowd. A late bloomer, he was small (5′6″) and thin, with glasses and curly, black hair trimmed short. Though generally in good health, he was bothered by asthma and hay fever, which necessitated weekly trips to Chicago for allergy shot treatments. "I was skinny and pasty and not physically developed," Bob later recalled, "I felt that I was a nerd."

Fortunately, in Bob's family, mental ability was prized far more than physical prowess. He was born in the south of Chicago, the only son of Jewish, working class parents. Morris, who was 41 when Bob was born, and Debra, then 33, had been married for nearly 15 years. Morris, a World War II veteran, ran a small packaging business on the South Side of the city. The couple had been trying to have a child for many years without success; and Debra's three sisters already had many children of their own. About three years before Bob's birth, the Rubins decided to adopt a child, a little girl from Eastern Europe whom they believed had lost her parents in the war. Unfortunately, less than a year after the adoption—which, as was common in the 1940's, was done without any formal papers—the girl's family arrived in the States and claimed her back. The Rubins fought for custody of the child in court, but lost.

Luckily, Debra became pregnant eighteen months later. Both parents were thrilled with their son. "He had all the love in the world," remarked Debra. Neither of the Rubins were highly educated, Debra had a high school diploma, while Morris had been forced to leave high school after his freshman year. They were anxious to give Bob the best educational opportunities. Before Bob reached school age, the family moved from their South Side neighborhood, which the Rubins felt was deteriorating, to the northern suburbs. Bob's intelligence, and particularly his aptitude for mathematics, were well in evidence by the time he reached high school, where he was an honor roll student. Morris and Debra felt tremendous pride in their son's scholastic achievements. "He does real well in school without even really trying," said Morris, "He can do his studying with one eye on the TV."

Though both avid readers, the Rubins were also keenly aware of the intellectual gulf that separated them and their son. "Neither my husband nor I are on a level with him," admitted Debra, "Sometimes it makes it hard for us to understand what he is talking about or learning."

Financially, the family struggled. As a small business owner, Morris worked long hours; during the latter half of Bob's high school, Debra joined him in the business. After a long day of work, both were often physically exhausted, particularly Morris, who had been injured in World War II and was later diagnosed with osteoarthritis. Bob was frequently left on his own to manage his time and plan activities. Morris faded even further into the background when it came to discipline, which was mainly left up to Debra, who, while admitting that she might be "too strict," at times, was deeply concerned with not spoiling her son. For his part, Bob felt extraordinarily close with his mother, though occasionally resentful of her tight leash. But his father's increasing infirmity caused him a great deal of stress. He felt particularly unhappy when he had to help Morris with basic physical tasks like putting on his shoes and socks. "I wish my parents had been younger," Bob remarked later.

Not surprisingly, Bob's parents were not fully aware of his conflicted feelings towards them, but they did notice that he was insecure outside the comfort zone of his intellectual achievements. Midway through high school, Bob had no close friends, and had never been on a date. He was convinced he was physically inadequate for athletics, and played no sports. Morris and Debra were somewhat concerned that their son had no close male buddies, and no girlfriends. "He seems to have a smaller group of friends than most," commented Morris. His seeming uninterest in his peers, however, was largely due to shyness: Bob did not view himself as attractive, and was far too timid to ask girls on dates. As such, he simply chose to stay away from the social situations that made him feel awkward and uncomfortable.

Rather than hanging out with friends or dating, Bob channeled his energy during high school into hobbies, reading, and part-time jobs. He loved tinkering with and fixing gadgets; racecars, aviation, TV and radio all fascinated him. He often read science fiction for pleasure, but also pushed himself to tackle more difficult works by modern authors like Hemingway.

By his senior year of high school, Bob began emerging from his shell. "I really came alive my senior year and started to date then," he said. Academically, he continued to sail, graduating in the top ten percent of his high school class. Having taken a greater interest in the world around him, his reading list broadened to include works by Freud, Marx, and Einstein. He also began to see himself as a nonconformist and rebel. "I liked to walk barefoot at night," he said. He hoped to "bum around the country," for a few months after high school.

But instead of bumming around, Bob stayed home and worked the summer after high school. He also regularly began dating a girl, Sharon, for the first time.

By his own admission, much of the relationship consisted of "making out." But Bob was unable to form an emotional bond with Sharon. Instead, he felt that she quickly became overly dependent on him, which he found unattractive. "It turned me off," he admitted. Sharon was upset by Bob's decision to break up with her, but although Bob found the process of breaking up with someone uncomfortable, he didn't miss the relationship.

After high school, Bob enrolled at the University of Illinois and moved to Champaign, 150 miles from home. He scored highly on the entrance exams and was granted nearly a year's worth of college credits as well as placement in all honors classes. Yet he was no longer the academic star that he was in high school, earning average grades his first year. Eye-opening college experiences were demanding their share of time. Caught up in the "turmoil of the late 60's," Bob began thinking about civil rights, Vietnam, and race relations. He was immediately sympathetic to the anti-war movement: "People who are for the war in Vietnam are close-minded and have a one-track mind," he said. Bob also took on greater financial responsibilities, parking cars in a garage in downtown Champaign to help pay his living expenses. He made new friends quickly, though he continued to shy away from deeper relationships with people.

As Bob gained financial independence, he began pulling away from his parents emotionally as well. With his arthritic condition becoming increasingly severe, Morris was no longer able to work, so Debra went back to work full-time to support the family. On visits home Bob argued with his father frequently. "Because Dad has nothing to do all day, he spends his time worrying about me," he griped. When father and son locked horns, Debra usually mediated and helped the pair reconcile.

Then, the summer after his freshman year of college, Bob fell in love for the first time. Judy "was the most interesting and outward girl I had ever known," he said. The relationship was intense. The couple even lived together for two months. But with Bob's social life increasingly expanding, he was able to meet other women easily, and found himself attracted to several of them. Judy, in turn, admitted that she had become interested in another man. After a series of fights, the couple split. But unlike his relationship with Sharon, Bob could not easily shrug it off. "I was down for weeks," he said.

In his second year of college, Bob moved into an apartment off-campus with several friends. The living arrangement allowed him even greater freedom to clarify his new political views in the company of like-minded friends. He also had an experience that changed the way he would relate to those around him for the rest of his life.

During his adolescence and early college years, Bob was unable to establish a deep emotional connection with his friends. One snowy night that fall, he pulled into a gas station and saw the attendant, an older man, inside the garage preparing to walk across the lot to collect the money for Bob's gas. Suddenly, Bob realized that the elderly man would suffer in the miserable weather, and quickly walked to meet him in the garage so he would not have to brave the storm. This moment of compassion was a revelation to him. As he later reflected: "The key to living is doing things not for what they get you, but because they're the good thing to do." After that night, he deliberately became more open and sensitive to the people around him.

That year, Bob grew closer to fellow students who shared his views on politics, leaving behind his old group of "straight" friends. Most of his new friends had long hair; he knew they would be considered "weird" by his parents and other adults. Yet he believed they were "good people, open people with good ideas." Discussing ideas—about the government, society, and politics—had become an important part of Bob's life. "The establishment is corrupt and ineffective," he claimed. Some of his views were contradictory. He admired anarchy, yet felt that people were basically "not good" and needed the control of government or administrative systems. Though he attended anti-war demonstrations, he considered them "ineffective and useless." Overall, his politics tended to support his admittedly "egoist" stance. "I don't want to go into the Armed Forces now, and I will do whatever I have to do so that I will not have to go," he said, "However, I may want to go, and if I do, then I will go."

After the upsetting break-up with Judy, Bob also "turned on" for the first time. Pot, and later LSD, felt liberating to him. "Acid socially deconditions you so you can experience feelings you never thought you could," he marveled. Bob became a regular pot smoker, believing it helped him establish deeper relationships with his friends. "I learned about how [other people] react emotionally . . . I observe how they react in society," he said. Bob admired friends whom he saw as outrageous and rebellious. One of his former roommates, who had dropped out of a series of schools and then joined the Navy, was later discharged following an arrest for marijuana possession. Bob was impressed with his antics, but in his own life, steered clear of becoming an "acid-head" or drop out. "I can't see going to those extremes," he admitted.

Nevertheless, Bob had come to view himself as something of a free spirit. "If you feel inside that something is right in matters of dress or sex, you should do whatever it is you have deemed to be right," he said. As a high school student, the thinking of worldly philosophers and writers had inspired him; midway through college, he had formed his own set of ideals. "People ought to be taught that the real meaning of life is not in possessions, but in peace of mind," he proclaimed.

Yet for all his idealistic talk, Bob had not yet found peace of mind in his own life. He was becoming increasingly disillusioned with academics. As an entering student, Bob had intended to major in math, but felt discouraged by the long proofs required in the upper-level classes. He switched to Physics, but encountered the same obstacle. His third department, Computer Science, pleased him more, though he still found most of the courses and teachers unmotivating.

A meaningful relationship with a woman also continued to elude him. As a sophomore, he had enough sexual experience to know that women found him attractive, though he attributed some of his success to the status symbol of having his own apartment. "Girls get horny, too," he remarked knowingly. Over the next two years, he had a series of unsatisfying relationships with women. One, a very beautiful fellow student named Karen, had been engaged to a man who was killed in Vietnam. Bob was unable to coax her out of her distress, and she left him for another student, who, in his view, didn't really care for her. Another romance that had blossomed out of a good friendship ended after the woman, Susan, spent a summer in San Francisco and began to think she might be gay. "She became too far out for me," he acknowledged, though the two remained good friends. While Susan was in San Francisco, Bob became involved with Pat, who was just seventeen. Pat seduced him one evening while he was listening to music. His lack of interest only fueled hers; rather than being put off by his rejections, she was impressed by his honesty. "All she wanted to do was jump into bed," he complained, "She was my curse." In his typically idealist fashion, Bob prided himself on not using women for sex as some of his male peers did. "A girl doesn't owe me anything for a date except courtesy," he declared proudly.

As he neared the end of college, Bob once again drew close to his mother. "When I first went to college, I got a big 'freedom thing' as far as my parents were concerned," he said. He was proud of his mother, who had been promoted to an office manager in the few years since she had gone back to work full-time. When Bob was home, he and Debra often stayed up talking until well into the night; he felt she was "like a friend." His relationship with his father, while less outwardly antagonistic, remained emotionally distant.

Despite the turmoil of Bob's college years, he continued to work hard in his part-time and summer jobs. During his last summer of college, he held a job at a large brokerage firm, which he believed would extend him a full-time offer after school. Though the "bumming around" he had dreamed of in high school would have been an option for him at that point, he no longer had the desire to do so. "The 'American Dream' still holds meaning for me," he said. He hoped to marry and raise a family someday. Bob believed that unlike previous generations of workers, he would not be motivated by money or success; instead, he wanted to work for enjoyment. Though college had been a time of transformation for him, he was impatient for it to end: "I'm waiting to get on with my life."

An objective observer looking at Bob at this point in his life might have wondered in what direction he was taking his life, whether he could pull himself together or whether he would just founder, unsure where he wanted to go. He seemed by turns idealistic and pragmatic, rebellious, and conforming. Yet there always was a core of strength in him, a sense that what seemed like lack of direction or foundering actually represented aspects of a quest for his own way in his own time. The direction of his life, as we shall see, was growth not psychopathology.

CARL

Of the three normal routes through adolescence, the tumultuous route was the one that showed functioning closest to that seen among disturbed teenagers. In 1975, these subjects were described as having recurrent self doubts accompanied by defensive braggadocio. They had escalating conflicts with their parents. They tended to mistrust adults. There was more depression and anxiety in this group than the other groups. Separating and individuating seemed to entail and even require turmoil. Adolescence was particularly difficult for them. At the same time, none suffered from marked clinical disturbance. They were in turmoil but had the psychological and emotional resources to get through and profit from adolescence, leaving them in a better position to cope with the demands of the next stage of life.

Carl was chosen in 1975 as an exemplar of this group. In high school, he seemed well adjusted. But family relationships were in turmoil, and in college, his adaptation seemed to take a turn for the worse. His story through his college years follows.

Reflecting on his adolescence as an adult, Carl Bender was hardly nostalgic. "My most vivid memories of high school are my parents fighting and my failure in school," he said. Born in Chicago, Carl was adopted when he was only four days old by Martin, who was a manager in the marketing department of a utilities company and Rosalie, who was a housewife. The Benders, whose five-year old marriage had been filled with conflict, hoped a child would bring harmony to the relationship. The reality proved very different. "Ever since I was aware of my parents, they were fighting," Carl said, "They had a horrible relationship, just horrible."

As a teenager, Carl was aware that there was a great deal of conflict in his household, but suppressed whatever concerns he may have had, commenting that he felt he was treated "justly" by his parents. As an adult, however, Carl recognized that his parents' tumultuous relationship had in fact caused him a great deal of emotional pain. "I don't want to blame anyone else for my shortcomings, but if I look objectively at my relationship with my parents, they screwed me up," he said.

From the beginning, Carl's parents seemed an unlikely pair. Both were originally from Indiana, but the similarities ended there. Carl's father, Martin, was raised in a strict middle-class Protestant household along with an adopted younger brother. He described himself as a rebel in his youth: "I cut classes, played dice, smoked at age 15," he said. Carl's mother, Rosalie, came from a Spanish, Mexican, and Indian background. She had grown up in an impoverished, chaotic household, with divorced parents who moved frequently. Rosalie briefly married when she was only 16, and had a son whom she gave up for adoption. She was working and attending community college when she met Martin, who was in school full time. Neither of them finished their college degrees. The Benders adopted Carl when Martin was 29 years old and Rosalie was supposedly 35—though, as Carl found out later, his mother was actually six years older than she claimed to be. "She lied about her age as long as I can remember," Carl said later.

By the time Carl was in elementary school, the relationship between his parents was rapidly degenerating. "My parents fought about anything and everything. They hated each other," said Carl. His father, Martin, emotionally withdrew from the family, and was frequently physically absent as well. "My dad did very little parenting," Carl said later, "He was an absent parent. My mom was the parent." Carl's mother had quit her sales job soon after Carl was adopted, and she never worked outside the home again. "My mother loved the security of the home," said Carl.

But if Rosalie viewed the Bender home as a sanctuary, she was unable to provide the same sense of security to her son. As Carl's father Martin drew away from the family, Rosalie's behavior became increasingly erratic, and she often took out her anger on her son. My mother was "spare the rod, spoil the child," said Carl later, "Some of my worst memories are what I now know was abuse. When somebody goes out and takes a rose switch off the bush and beats your backside or grabs your father's belt and hits you with it, that's abuse. I didn't even know it at the time. I thought everybody got hit. Now I know better."

The Benders were also intensely critical of their son. "The school considered holding Carl back in kindergarten- there was a question about immaturity," said Martin, his father, "I allowed them to make the decision to put him ahead, and I have always felt I made a mistake and that perhaps he's always been a little behind as a result." Martin also did not believe his son had the capacity to excel in sports. "He is very good at golf and bowling, but as soon as there is any physical contact, he backs off," he said. Later, Carl realized that the sting of his parents' criticism hurt badly. "If I had to rate my parents on a scale of one to five on how supportive they were, I'd say a zero," he said, "I never felt like I did anything right."

Even without the support of his parents, Carl was naturally an active, amiable person. "Carl has an unparalleled zest for life—he goes to bed and wakes up singing," remarked his father. Carl knew he was adopted from a very young age, though his mother told him many different stories about his birth parents ("I heard my father left my mother, my mother died at birth, your mother didn't want you— I must have heard 8, 10, 12 different stories," he later recalled). But on the whole, he emerged with no bad feelings about his adoption. "My parents must have done that right," Carl reflected as an adult, "I've always known my whole life and it never bothered me."

As a teenager, Carl often coped with his difficult parental relationships by turning a blind eye to the reality of the situation. Indeed, at age sixteen, he presented an idealized version of his relationship with his father: "My father is a good friend and we play golf and ball together," he said. And he had a great deal of respect for his father's position as family breadwinner. "When I was in high school I thought my father made more money than God," Carl recalled. He also respected his father's intelligence. "Although my dad did not have a lot of formal education, he was very smart," Carl said later, "My mom had no formal education and did not educate herself. She was not smart. Although she seemed street smart at times, I never thought she was intelligent at all."

Developing a full life outside the home also helped Carl cope with his parents' criticism and physical abuse. When Carl was sixteen, his father remarked: "Carl is extremely gregarious and likes to be with a group." As an adult, Carl had pleasant memories of his high school social life. "I had a lot of friends and my house was the meeting place, it was kind of fun," he said. Carl also developed an extremely close bond with his paternal grandfather. "He was a great guy," he said later, "I trusted his judgment." But Carl's relationships outside his home could not make up for the damage that his parent's constant disapproval had wrought on his self-esteem. "If someone gave me a million dollars, I'd probably spend it on the wrong things," he said.

By Carl's senior year, the reality of his father's drinking and absenteeism could no longer be ignored. Although Carl was not fully aware of it at the time, his father was having a serious extramarital affair. "At this point, my relationship with my dad was nonexistent;" Carl said later, "He wasn't around. He was either working hard or playing around. Out drinking, out with the guys, with his girlfriend." Once he had neared his adult height and weight, Carl no longer had to endure abuse from his mother "I got too big for her to hit me," Carl said, "I would have hit back."

As an adult, Carl frankly stated that he felt his mother's behavior had driven his father to have affairs. "I wouldn't have come home to that either," he remarked. But as a seventeen year old, Carl felt sympathetic towards his mother. "She knew about my father's relationship outside the marriage and she really crucified him for it," Carl said later, "She turned me against him somewhat, I was on her side. "The harmony between Carl and his mother did not last long, however. "I felt bad for her, but she was still nuts," he said, "At least my dad was rational. Whatever he did, at least I could make sense out of it. My mom was too weird."

Though bright and capable, Carl never excelled in school. "His tests indicate that he is brighter than average, and he should be doing substantially better than he is," said his father. Carl's parents blamed their son's low grades on the fact that he was slightly younger than the other students in his class, and therefore "immature." "Basically, Carl is a playboy and he only wants to play. It has affected his school work," said his father. In reality, Carl did not have the confidence that he could succeed academically, particularly in subjects that he found boring or difficult. As a way of saving face, he chose not to work up to his abilities. "Every report card talked about me not applying myself," he said, "I'd get the most bizarre report cards ever—one of everything, A, B, C, D and F. I'd think, well, that's cool, I've never seen that before. But if it was something I liked, I did great." Later, Carl recognized that as a teenager, he had subconsciously hoped that his chronic under-performance would be hurtful to his parents. "I wasn't a bad kid. I was lazy," Carl said, "When

I sit back and look . . . I think I thought I was punishing my parents. Give them more grief . . . like if you think I'm bad now, just wait . . . "

By the middle of high school, Carl was very interested in girls. "I like their figures," he commented shyly. Carl's parents were unaware that their son was interested in girls. When Carl was fifteen, his father described him as "unconscious of the opposite sex." But in reality, Carl simply did not feel at all confident about dating. "In high school, I didn't think girls liked me," he said later. Though he often "daydreamed" about girls, he denied having the desire for a girlfriend. "It isn't important," he claimed.

Religion was another constant source of conflict in the Bender household. When Carl was in high school, his mother Rosalie, who had been raised Catholic, converted to Jehovah's Witness, and became an ardent practitioner. "My mother went to church constantly, 4 or 5 days a week," Carl recalled. Carl's father Martin, a Protestant, was disdainful of his wife's newfound religious fervor. "There was a lot of turmoil, a lot of religious turmoil in the house. I didn't want to be involved." For his part, Carl simply felt alienated from all religion. "God knows what my religious background was," he said, "I'd call it Heinz 57—a mix of everything."

During high school, Carl hoped to someday study law, despite his poor grades. But when it came time to make post high school plans, the community college near his home was his best and most affordable option. Carl continued to live at home with his parents, which strained their already difficult relationship near the breaking point. "I should move out, but I can't afford it," he said, "The price at home is right." By Carl's sophomore year, he and his parents had "absolutely no relationship," he said. The death of his beloved paternal grandfather seemed to finalize his complete alienation from his family. "My mother never tells me who calls, she just completely disassociates herself from me," he said.

With his home life still a struggle, Carl found it hard to enjoy college. "I hated college and hated living at home," he said later, "I pretty much never even came home." A business major, Carl's lack of confidence in his academics skills continued to haunt him as it had in high school, and he obtained a 'C' average for his freshman and sophomore year. Emotionally, Carl found it easier to constantly underachieve than undergo the occasional disappointment of not succeeding. "My grades are just about right for me—I don't work too hard," he admitted. Carl found it easier to be successful in sports, like golf, or card games. He had also discovered a passion for gambling. "I have a lucky streak," he said.

Another source of pleasure for Carl in his college years was his girlfriend, Susan, whom he began dating as a freshman. "I was attracted to her because I liked her legs," he joked, "No, really, it was her brain. I looked at her and said, there is a smart girl. And it was also her honesty, her compassion for friends and family." Though Carl had some sexual experience during his freshman year, Susan was the first woman he slept with regularly. "She lives alone, so it's easy," he said.

Despite the difficulties he had encountered in his teenage years, Carl's innate strength and good-natured spirit frequently enabled him to overcome his negative emotions. "When I get anxious or depressed I play golf," he said, "That pretty much takes care of it." But college had not entirely enabled Carl to shake off the effects of his tumultuous teenage years. As a sophomore, he had little ability to envision himself as a successful, independent adult, and he had few career ambitions. That year, he took a part-time office job selling insurance, which he found he enjoyed. "I might like to be a salesman," he said vaguely. He also considered joining the military. "A lot of my friends are in the Army," he said, "I'll go if I'm drafted."

During Carl's junior year, he married Susan and dropped out of college at the end of the semester. He began working full-time at the insurance sales job, but was notified shortly thereafter that he was being drafted. Carl's attitude was neither enthusiastic nor defiant. "My birth year was the first year of the lottery. That's the way it was," he said. The Army had temporarily rescued him from the adult pressure of having to make further educational or career decisions. At age 22, Carl was content to cede control of the direction of his life, while emotionally, he continued to drift.

In 1975, it was commented about Carl that at age 22, he had not yet learned to cope well with his feelings, emotions, and fantasy life. He had many self-doubts and was undergoing a moderately severe identity crisis. His emotions were in flux. But it was noted that he had considerable resources for coping with his social milieu. He had psychological resources to draw from such as use of humor and pragmatism. It was suggested that the stability of his functioning and self-contentment in the future remained in doubt. How in fact he did turn out will be discussed in a later chapter.

The stories of the three young men described in this chapter exemplify qualitatively different ways of going through or adapting to adolescence. The commonality among these three young men was the resilience and depth of inner resources they brought to what can be a difficult period of life. Tony seemed to have everything going for him. Bob lurched and skidded and then straightened up again. Carl seemed to be in a downward spin after high school, reeling from inner tumult a difficult family situation had visited upon him. But all three had this in common: none went into an irreversible downward course involving, for example, alcohol or drug addiction, clinical depression, or serious criminal behavior. There may have been turmoil, self-doubt, and confusion. But, in the end, they emerged from adolescence ready for the next turn in their lives, ready to meet the challenges ahead.

NOTE

1. We are grateful to Cybelle Weisser, M.A., for writing this chapter.

Chapter 5

Against All Odds
How the Late Middle-Age Study Was Done

The story of how data were obtained from our subjects at age 48 should be called "against all odds". This stage of the study was initiated and shepherded by an interested individual (Marjorie Kaiz Offer, the second author) who did not have formal training in psychiatric or psychological research. It's funding was atypical. Moreover, the recruitment and participation of 94% of the living subjects is unprecedented.

This phase of the project began with human curiosity. In 1990, the senior author had changed professional positions. He had left his medical home of 30 years, Chicago's Michael Reese Hospital and Medical Center and traveled cross-town to Northwestern University Medical School to become a Professor of Psychiatry and Behavioral Sciences. Office space at Northwestern was at a premium so several of his file cases and storage boxes had been moved to the basement of his home. Four boxes contained the data on the 73 teenage lives.

Soon after the materials arrived, the second author reorganized the basement. She came across the cartons and began to read the old interviews. She read the words of boys who had dreams about the future, marrying, and having families. They liked girls and sports. She read interviews with the mothers and the fathers whose pride and love for their sons jumped from the pages. With each of the boys' folders, she became increasingly curious about the fate of these men.

She approached the senior author with what she considered a simple and exciting idea: to find all the subjects and re-interview them in mid-life. The young men were interesting and she was intrigued about how they had turned out. Her professional background was in journalism and non-profit marketing so her interest was in the human aspect of the story.

This idea was met with skepticism. The senior author pointed out the immense hurdles. Since there were initially only 73 men, he noted, to have useful statistical information, the response rate had to be over 90%. He stressed the difficulty in finding all the subjects and the seeming impossibility of convincing over 90% to participate.

The second author was not discouraged. She approached colleagues of the first author for advice. She particularly valued the opinion of Kenneth Howard, Professor of Psychology at Northwestern University who had worked with the senior author since 1963. He thought the project was interesting but expressed skepticism about how achievable it was. However, he offered whatever support he could give.

The second author began to look for the 73 men in November of 1991. In order to succeed in their recruitment, there had to be a careful step-by-step plan to hold their interest from the first point of contact until the actual interview was completed. When we began the search for the subjects, we did not have funding or a completed research instrument, but we did have a plan.

Using investigative techniques, we began the project of locating every subject and his home phone number. In fact, in the end, we were invariably able to do so. Also, after speaking to whomever answered, we explained that we were calling from Northwestern University Medical School. This gave us immediate entree and bought us a few seconds to quickly tell about the return of Dr. Offer and the study.

We then explained to whomever we spoke that we were trying to locate, for example, John Smith the son of Tom and Jane Smith who had graduated from XYZ high school in 1966. If they asked why, we explained that we were trying to get in contact with Mr. Smith as he had participated in a medical research project for eight years about 30 years ago.

If by chance Mr. Smith himself answered, we would tell him that we would be sending him a letter. We finished by reconfirming his address. At no time did we ever ask him whether we could write to him; we always assumed that he would respond positively to this simple request. By design, nothing was asked of the subject during the first contact, so there was never an opportunity to say no at the beginning of the process.

We prepared the following letter:

303 East Ohio—Suite 550   **Daniel Offer, M.D.**
Chicago, Illinois 60611   Professor of Psychiatry and
(312) 908-8836   Director of Adolescent Research

NORTHWESTERN UNIVERSITY MEDICAL SCHOOL
Department of Psychiatry and Behavioral Sciences

June 4, 1991

Dear Mr._____:

In 1962 I began a study through Michael Reese Hospital of normal adolescence. With the cooperation of_____High School, you were one of 73 students who participated in our study. At that time, virtually nothing was known about the experiences of normal adolescents and their families. Funded by the Federal government, project staff and I periodically met and talked to each student about their current life at that time. Members of my staff also talked with parents. Two books resulted from our study, documenting the experiences of normal teenagers. One of those entitled, *The Psychological World of the Teenager* (New York: Basic Books, 1969) became a landmark text in informing parents, educators and mental health professionals about the experience of normal teens.

This fall it will have been 29 years since we began the study. I think it would be important and timely to speak once again with each of the participants in the study. We will be contacting you in the near future to discuss this.

Cordially,
Daniel Offer, M. D.
Professor of Psychiatry

If we had not called in advance to reconfirm an address, we always included an explanation of how we found their address. Our goal was to present nothing threatening in our reappearance from the past.

The letter was a business letter and we felt we needed to warm it up. We decided to attach a smiling picture of the senior author to each letter. This communication was to announce the return of an old friend. We photographed the senior author with big glasses and a moustache, both of which have disappeared since the project's beginning in 1991. With great conviction, we ordered 73 copies of the picture (see page 42).

We then had to decide who would next speak to each man, what should we ask of him, and what should we tell him. Since the senior author signed the letter, it was logical that he should be the one to call. But after one practice call, we felt that his skepticism about the project was evident. By default the second author became the voice the subjects grew to know. Luckily the last name of each of us, Offer, helped establish trust easily.

What to ask of them was tricky. We didn't want to ask for a commitment to participate. That could invite a negative response. We decided to simply ask if they would consider participating. We did not need or want a definitive answer. We just

Figure 1. The photograph of Daniel Offer attached to the first letter to each subject.

wanted them to think about it. We told them that this would be an opportunity to make a contribution to medical science and make history. We were trying to capture their imagination.

Since the process of finding the subjects was going to be a lengthy one, we developed a bi-annual newsletter to keep them up-to-date on how we were doing in our hunt to locate the 73 men and report on the project's development. The newsletter was designed to hold their interest, and hopefully build their desire to participate. They received this newsletter every six months along with a change-of-address form. This last item was essential, as we didn't want to spend months, in some cases years, to locate someone, just to have him move and disappear.

In trying to locate the subjects, we used the fact that all the subjects had two facts in common. First, they all had been born in approximately 1948. Second, we knew that they all had gone to one of two Chicago suburban high schools. We did not have their birth dates nor did we have their social security numbers, the two critical facts needed to find someone in the United States today (while their birth dates were available 28 years ago, those data were lost in the move from Reese to Northwestern). We did have all their old files, which held clues about each man. Sometimes the interviews revealed where their mother or father worked, what their siblings' names were, where they went to college, if they went to the army, or some other snippet of information.

Finding people was something we had never before undertaken. The internet in 1991 was in its infancy. Going on line to find someone was not an option, so other time consuming methods had to be used. The project was based out of our home. We always had three active searches going at one time. Over time we had a separate pile of difficult ones to locate, ones that took years to accomplish.

We began by ordering nine new Chicago area phones books, covering the metropolitan area. The easiest approach was to locate those who had grown up in the suburbs and had never left the area. First we would find the subject's name and call everyone with that name. If that didn't work, we would, if they were listed, call the fathers and the mothers, whose names were in the old file. They were now in their 60's, 70's and 80's and many had never moved away. Significantly, they had been involved in the study and remembered it well. The senior author originally had the parents help determine whether they believed their sons were normal and whether they should be included in the sample. Later, almost all the mothers and fathers had been individually interviewed. All the parents had been fully cooperative. In the current time frame, most gave us the address and phone number of their son. A few checked with their children first. Sometimes the local phone canvass would turn up brothers, sisters or more distant relatives. Slowly the list of people we found grew and each person said that they would think about participating. No one said no.

Sometimes the old files gave us other clues about the subject's parents, so we hunted for the parent hoping they were alive. One subject's father had worked at the time of the original study for a Chicago institution as a maintenance man. Luckily the father worked there another twenty years, retired and was receiving his pension from them. The company forwarded our letter to the parent, who sent us their son's address and telephone number. Various books gave us ideas on how to locate people (Culligan, 1991; Ferraro, 1989; and Johnson, 1990).

We wrote each of the superintendents of the two original high schools, explaining the project and requesting a chance to review their alumnae lists in order to obtain addresses. One high school did not have any official file. The other requested a copy of the 1961 original study approval, which we were able to locate in the old cartons and then gave us access to the alumni list. The list provided addresses of subjects, or, sometimes their siblings, who led us to their brothers.

Subjects already contacted also helped. One man wanted to know how we were finding the other men. We told him that his high school was the one that did not maintain an alumni list. He then sent a copy of his 20th high school reunion program with names and addresses of classmates, some of whom we were seeking. He also put us in touch with a classmate who kept an unofficial list of where people were. She sent her complete mailing list to us. Note that we never asked for the address of a specific person, since we could not breach confidentiality.

Another route involved the alumni office of a college or university. Most would give us the last address on file. Others would forward our letter to the subject.

Our biggest search success was in finding one subject who had no traditional address or phone number. When we began to look for him, his old file showed that he had transferred to a new university in his sophomore college year. The alumni office of his first college provided his, as far as they know, last known address, which was in New Orleans, Louisiana. After calling information in New Orleans, we found he was not listed. However there was one listing for a woman with the same last name. Our next call was to her. She turned out to be his 80-year-old mother who remembered the study. She reported that her son lived on a fifty-foot boat in the Caribbean Sea. We then placed a call to the U.S. Coast Guard, who located his boat off the shore of Mexico allowing us to place a ship-to-shore call to our subject, who continued in the study.

Other clues in the file helped turn up subjects. We knew from the high school records that one subject's father had died when he was in high school. The boy was Jewish and we knew that once a year a notice is sent to a family member to remind them of the Yahrzeit, the anniversary of the day of death, when a prayer is said in the local synagogue. All the synagogues in the area of the high school were canvassed until we found the one where the family had been a member decades before. They were still sending out the Yahrzeit notice to a family member, who led us to our subject.

The teenagers themselves left clues in their adolescent files. Two of them had planned to become physicians. The local library maintained a reference book listing all physicians by specialty in the U.S. They were easily found.

Another old file had a letter sent from a subject while serving in Vietnam in 1969. It gave our subject's rank, serial number and last address. We submitted this information to the Vietnam Veterans of America, and requested it be listed in the locator service of their publication. Following the listing of the information, a reader sent us a list of eight men with the same name in the U.S. and their phone numbers. We started calling them, one by one. Number four was our subject. When he picked up the phone, he was cautious until we made reference to his grandmother whom he had lived with in high school. With that, he relaxed. He continued in the study.

Sometimes fate was on our side. We located one man's local address in 1992; however, his phone number was unlisted. Sticking to our plan, we wrote him our standard letter with a form to please send his unlisted number with the understanding it would be held in the strictest confidence. He did not respond. A year later, after checking with information and confirming that the number was still unlisted, we wrote again. There still was no response. In 1994 and 1995 we made our annual call to information. In 1996 we called information again and astonishingly they gave us his phone number. Immediately we called. The subject was initially irate. He had always requested his phone be unlisted. We explained the way we had found the number and told our medical research story. He too continued in the study and his phone number was immediately unlisted again. There was never a real explanation for that telephone company lapse in privacy.

The "impossible" people needed a special approach. The *Chicago Tribune* each Sunday ran a story called "First Person." On December 15, 1991, the story focused on Michael Sussman a probate researcher. The headline read, "We're contacted when someone has died and an heir is being sought." Michael Sussman was described as having a law degree from Northwestern University. We thought that perhaps our common Northwestern University ties would help us. In addition to the senior author's having an appointment at Northwestern's Medical School, the second author was a graduate of the University's Medill School of Journalism.

In April of 1992, the senior author wrote Michael Sussman about the project and our desire to reconnect with the 73 men. We requested a phone consultation about the project with the second author. When we called, Mr. Sussman was friendly and gracious. The second author asked whether he would consider helping with the project. He offered to help. Two years passed. We called again, explaining that we had found almost all the subjects. Mr. Sussman helped us, pro bono, locate the last, most difficult to reach, subjects.

It took over the five years, until 1996, to gather information about all 73 subjects. Unfortunately, during our quest, we learned that two of these subjects had died. We learned of the death of one in March of 1992 when we called his mother. We had found her number in the phone book. She remembered the study immediately. She told us her son had died eight years ago at the age of 35 after having been sick for more than a decade with melanoma. We received the information about the death of the second subject through a call to his father's office. He had died of leukemia the year before, we were told.

At some point, curiously, we became concerned that everyone located might agree to participate. We thought a 100 percent response rate would appear peculiar. This problem, however, was solved by the non-participation of four men. In one case, the man's wife objected. One was in prison for white-collar crime; he wanted to participate but could not obtain permission to do so. A third was on probation for marijuana possession and was wary of any contact. The fourth joked that he would participate in the "old-age" phase of the study, not this one.

In sum, by 1996 after five years, we had found and contacted the 71 surviving men of the original sample of 73. They lived in 24 states as well as the District of Columbia and on the Caribbean Sea. Sixty-seven subjects agreed to and did participate in our study.

We had known that what we wanted to do would be expensive. While we were searching for the men in the first half of the 1990's, we were also searching for funding. Our natural funding source should have been an agency for the U.S. government. Such agencies had underwritten the first eight years of the study, from the fall of 1962 to the fall of 1971.

But times had changed in America. The Women's Movement, affirmative action, and demographic realities had altered government guidelines. The study and its subjects were demographically limited. They originally were selected using opportunity samples of normal boys in two incoming freshman classes in 1962. The samples did not reflect the demographics of the 1962 U.S. adolescent population. Likewise, our subjects were not representative of late 1990's middle-aged U.S. adults. The sample only had one Hispanic and two African Americans. There were no Asian Americans or American Indians. Most importantly, there were no women. It should be noted that originally the senior author had been advised not to include women. Colleagues had warned him that grant reviewers from the National Institutes for Mental Health might consider it risky for a 31-year-old male researcher to interview teenage girls. It should be noted too that, aside from the prohibitive cost, studies of representative samples, randomly selected from the total population, have their own very serious limitations, including, often, high rates of refusal to participate, which tends to obviate their claimed representativeness.

As a Northwestern University employee, the senior author was required to obtain permission from the university and the hospital to approach potential donors. The development department of each serves as a gatekeeper for their institution, determining the priority of each project, and assigning prospects for funding. We were informed that we could not approach, without their approval, a local foundation where we were known or an individual whom we knew personally and thought would be interested. Our project was not a university or hospital priority, it turned out, and, all but one funding prospect that we personally identified had been assigned other priorities. That prospect was not willing to provide funding.

Northwestern University did give permission to approach national foundations interested in mental health. There were nine foundations that seemed to be appropriate. We sent letters of inquiry or full proposals to all nine. What followed was a series of refusals of consideration or rejections. A follow-up study of normal men clearly was not a local or national research priority.

By the fall of 1993, we realized that there would be no outside funding. Most medical research is funded in the U.S. today. Faced with this financial impasse, we decided to join an elite group of scientists, who are self-funded. Several of these individuals were featured in a report in *Science Magazine* (1998), which highlighted the pluses and the minuses of undertaking research this way. On the positive side, we had the freedom to pursue challenging, creative work. In the article Nobelist Joshua Lederberg of Rockefeller University in New York City, points out one of the big minuses: "One of the problems is you lose external validation. That can be as important as the money."

One evening in the summer of 1996, we were out with our friends, Thomas F. and Sue Pick and Jane and Muller Davis. Jane, who is as curious as she is intelligent, quizzed the senior author on every aspect of the research. She was intrigued by the project, its research protocol and its lack of funding. Thomas F. Pick, a Chicago philanthropist and businessman, quietly listened. That conversation piqued Thomas F. Pick's interest and he consequently underwrote a three-year $30,000 grant. We obtained our external validation.

In moving ahead, we did have a powerful intellectual as well as financial ally, in our friend, Kenneth Howard. He gave his time and support of his staff for this project gratis. He would continue to do this for ten years of the project, until his death in 2000. Northwestern University itself was our second ally with its institutional support.

In the years that followed, we overcame each financial hurdle. When we did the face-to-face interviews, we used free venues such as conference rooms of public libraries. When we had to travel for interviews, different friends graciously shared their homes, and at times, their offices with us. A University of Chicago graduate student, Susan Taber, offered to do almost half of the interviews. Each interview had to be both coded for the computer and transcribed. Ken Howard and his staff helped considerably with the coding and transcribing of the interviews.

During the first half of the 1990's, while the hunt for the subjects and the funding went on, we debated about the research instrument. We had about four hours to gather all the information. This was the maximum amount of time that the subject and the interviewer could sustain in one interview. While we had a time restraint, in fact every aspect of their lives was interesting to us.

The primary question we wanted to answer was whether the subjects were still psychologically normal. Beyond that, we had no specific theory that we set out to test. We supported the law of unintended consequences of scientific discovery, also known as serendipity. An example of this is Dr. John Enders' work in the late nineteen forties. He was attempting to grow the mumps virus and found the method that ultimately proved essential to producing the polio vaccine. Rather than focus on one thesis, we decided to throw a wide net and see what turned up.

We debated the method to use in the interview. Did we want to gather only statistical or quantitative information or did we want to find out their life stories and draw conclusions from their commentaries? In the end, we thought this rare opportunity demanded that we use both, a survey method to allow statistics to be performed and a narrative method for life stories.

We achieved this by doing the interview twice within the four hours. During the first two hours, we asked questions that required only one or two word answers. This was followed by two paper and pencil tests, the Symptom Checklist-90-Revised, and a form we created, which asked questions about their health, income and sexuality. During the second two hours of the interview, we repeated the first sequence, this time eliciting a description of their lives by asking probing, open-ended questions.

This was a large amount of information to gather in a relatively short period of time. To make information gathering as blind as possible, old files were not reviewed before the interview. Since it took years from the time the subject was located until the time of the interview, the old information was forgotten by the second author, who interviewed more than half the subjects. Because it was such a lengthy interview, food was essential. We always served a meal during the data collection. We took their order in advance customizing lunch or dinner. All interviews were taped and transcribed.

A call came in May of 1995. The subject on the high seas in the Carribean was going to be on shore the next week. Thus began the gathering of the data. The interview stage of the project lasted a year and nine months, finishing in February of 1997. It was one thing to find them. We anticipated that getting at least 90% to actually do the interview would be the difficult part. They were all in their late 40's, very busy people with work and family obligations. Several did not want to meet, but we were always patient, waiting at times for over a year to schedule a meeting. We always maintained a positive attitude, even when we crossed the country by plane, railroad and taxi and a subject did not show up for his appointment. We were sincerely empathic, offering to return at their convenience.

Sometimes the dedication of the men gave us the inspiration to labor on. One of the subjects had fallen and broken five vertebrae in his back two days before the scheduled interview. We had flown to meet him for the appointment not knowing of his accident. He, of course, did not show up for his interview. He rescheduled for the next day, however, the day he was returning home from the hospital.

The interviews as performed had a common rhythm. Often the subject was nervous when he arrived. Many had known about the follow-up phase of study for years and had been waiting for the interview. Many had built up a sense of anticipation and were eager for the meeting. At the beginning, the first few minutes were always a little tense. The men as teens had been selected because they were "normal" and many were concerned about whether they still qualified to be in the group. After the first 10 minutes, the subject usually would relax, perhaps after the old research alliance had activated.

During 1996 and into 1997, we interviewed one subject after another, travel-ing the country. We became excited as we approached that magical 90% number. On February 3, 1997, we completed the final interview. Sixty-seven men or 94% per cent of the living subjects continued in the middle age phase of this study and had been interviewed, . . . against all odds.

Chapter 6

Men in Late Middle Age
The Texture of Their Lives

RESULTS

Data were analyzed with respect to various areas salient to the life of adult males. These areas included: work; religion; leisure; relationship with parents; siblings; wives or other partners; children; continuity in family constellation; mental health; physical health; alcohol or other substance use; sexuality; and memory. Analyses were primarily descriptive, presenting information as to the ways these men interact with and feel about their world.

WORK

Few would disagree with Freud's assertion that work is of central importance for each person. A man's profession, or how he earns his living, is part of the core of his life. On meeting a man, one of the first questions many of us ask is, "And what do you do?" Not only does a man spend approximately half of his waking hours working, he carries what he does like a shield, or banner that defines him.

In this section, we will describe the type of work these men did, how work affected them, what their experiences were like, and what they thought of their work.

Right after high school or after college, 22 of the 67 subjects served in the Armed Forces of the USA, the plurality in the Navy. Thirteen of them served more than three years. Five of them served in Vietnam. The rest of them were stationed in various places throughout the world. (See Figures 1, 2, 3, and 4.)

Table 1. Work

Socio-Economic Profile of the Men	
Professional/Technical	54%
Managers/Officials	19%
Proprietors	5%
Clerical	3%
Sales	3%
Craftsmen/foremen	6%

Military experience had a strong influence on the lives of those who served. The five men who served in Vietnam suffered various traumatic experiences. It is of interest to note that the majority of the fathers of our subjects served in the Armed Forces during WWII.

All of these men except one were employed at the time they were interviewed. The one person who was not working had made enough money to be able to retire.

The current socio-economic profiles of the men can be seen in Table #1. It shows that a majority of the men are professional or technical in status. The income of our subjects is in the upper middle class range. In 1994, thirty-nine percent have incomes of more than $100,000 and only six percent have an income of less than $35,000. (See Figure 5.) The U.S. Census Bureau mean household income for 1995 by fifths was the following: lowest fifth, $8,300; second fifth, $20,400; third fifth, $34,100; fourth fifth, $52,400; and highest fifth is $109,400.

When we look at the married men as a subgroup, we see that 50% are in the professional and technical social class compared to 41% of their wives, who are working outside the home. Twenty-four percent are managers or officials compared to 11% of their working wives. Thirty percent of the wives do not work outside the home; in other words, they are housewives. (See Figure 6.)

Since our subjects were the first baby boom generation, their fathers all experienced the Depression of the nineteen thirties. It is, therefore, of interest to compare our subjects to their fathers along two variables, level of education and socioeconomic status.

The data shows that 58% of the subjects stayed in the same social class as their fathers. Twenty-seven percent moved up in their socio-economic status while fifteen percent moved down. When we compared the educational achievement of the subjects and their fathers, the differences were not significant. On the whole, the subjects have only slightly better education than their fathers. (Any data not shown in the tables are available from the authors.)

Another comparison of interest pertains to the relationship between class standing at the end of high school and income at age 48. Prior research has a strong relationship between class standing and future occupational status. Consistent with prior research, our subjects who were top students did better economically in the market place. (See Figure 7.)

We turn next to the kind of experience our subjects have in their work. Forty-five percent have been doing the same kind of work all their adult life. Thirty-three percent have done the same type of work between ten and twenty years. Only three percent have been doing their current type of work for less than one year. (See Figure 8.)

On the whole, our subjects like the work they are doing. On a scale from 1 to 6, where 6 is "like work very much" and 1 is "dislike work very much," 73% endorsed either a 5 or 6. The vast majority, 76%, felt that they have a good balance between family life and their work. This is a striking finding since one hears so often that individuals feel that they do not have enough time for their families. (See Figures 9 and 10.)

Slightly more than half (52%) of the men believe that they are using all of their talents and abilities in the work setting. Most of our subjects (69%) are satisfied with the fringe benefits that they received.

In regard to any perceived changes in their work milieu, 67% say that the work place had changed significantly in recent years. They did not mention the entry of women and minorities into their work setting as having appreciably changed their jobs. Subjects mentioned a number of factors that did have an impact on their work. These factors, which make the work place more intense, included downsizing, political machinations in the work place, the emergence of competitive company buyouts, unions, security in the work place, and the economy in general.

Since adulthood, 45% of our group had had the experience of being un-employed for more than one month. Sixty-six percent of whose who had been unemployed at least that long had been either fired or laid off. Twenty-seven percent quit their job because they were dissatisfied. Of those who had been un-employed for at least a month, 67% had the experience of being unemployed for up to six months while 30% had the experience of being unemployed for more than six months. Most people were satisfied with how they resolved their being unemployed. (See Figures 11, 12, and 13.)

Clearly, these subjects like the work they are doing. They are satisfied with their lot in life. They do not sit at home dreaming of a different life.

Religion

The religions of our subjects were Protestant 57%, Jewish 21%, Catholic 9%, and Other or None 12%.

When in their freshman year of high school, 42% of the subjects reported going to church or synagogue every week, while 35% reported attending church or synagogue infrequently. Twenty-three percent said they did not attend religious services at all.

When asked about this subject as adults, the men had a different report. Twenty-two percent went to church or synagogue once a week or more; 36% attended services less than once a week; and 39% did not attend church at all. These data indicate that over the years, our subjects have become less invested in attending church or synagogue. (See Figures 14 and 15.)

Leisure and Social Life

On the whole, our subjects are hard-working individuals. When asked whether they feel that they have enough leisure time, there was an almost equal split between those who answered in the affirmative and those who said no. (See Figure 16.)

How much leisure time do they have available to them? Our data show that 73% have more than 10 hours of leisure time available to them each week; another 25% have between 5 and 10 hours of leisure time available to them each week.

When asked how they spend their leisure time, only 27% of these men specifically mentioned spending leisure time with their family. The men also mentioned sports, traveling, work around the house, watching television, and going to the movies. Reported leisure activities also included things like vacationing, sports with peers, playing music, collecting antiques, enjoying hobbies, exploring cyberspace, breeding fish, volunteering in the community, reading and spending time with friends.

The vast majority of these subjects, 81%, take vacations. They do a variety of things while on vacation. Most of them like to travel (67%). They also engage in athletic activities (53%). Some take restful vacations. Their activities include visiting with friends and relatives. Eleven percent mentioned work around the house. Nine percent reported having taken work related vacations. (See Figures 17, 18, and 19.)

Their social circle is relatively large. Fifty-eight percent said that they have five or more friends and 34% had 2 to 4 people in their close circle of friends. Sixty-nine percent said that they have a "best friend."

Slightly more than half of our subjects (52%) said that they socialize with people at work, mostly co-workers. There was a clear separation across levels of authority, which differentiated the lines of authority at work. Only 10% socialize with their supervisors, and 12% socialize with supervisees. When they socialize with people at work, they go out to the movies or engage in or watch sports. Occasionally, they go out drinking with a colleague. A few of them go to company-sponsored events. When the subjects were asked whether they felt close to the coworkers they socialize with, 86% said they did. Seventy-two percent of the men who socialized with coworkers said that they can confide in them. Most subjects socialize with people on the same level as themselves.

Altogether having fun and relaxing was definitely part of these men's lives. It expresses itself in different ways, but the goal is the same.

THE SUBJECTS AND THEIR PARENTS

In their adolescence, the majority of our subjects got along well with their parents, as was described earlier. Our data show that the positive nature of this relationship continued into late middle age.

As adolescents, our subjects had reported that when they grew up they wanted to have a life similar to the one they saw that their parents had. Perhaps they wanted to make more money than their fathers, but on the whole, they wanted to duplicate the life of their parents. Their parents, likewise, were very proud of their children. On the whole, they got along well with them, and what was even more important, liked them. We were surprised that the vast majority of the mothers, when asked to describe their sons, told us that their son was a "very good boy." The parents had no significant problems with them and, in general, whether they were A, B, or C students did not matter to the parents, as long as they passed all their subjects.

When we saw the subjects again at age 48, 76% of the mothers were still living. Those still alive ranged in age from 65 to 91. Of the mothers still alive, 90% were healthy and living independently, while 10% were not well and were not able to live independently. Four percent were being taken care of by family members, 4% were in nursing homes, and 2% were being taken care of through other arrangements. (See Figures 20 and 21.)

It was of interest to note how often the subjects keep in contact with their mothers. Sixteen percent talk to their mothers daily, 57% weekly, 23% monthly or less, and 4% have no contact with their mothers at all. (See Figure 22.)

Fifty-one percent of the subjects said they were very satisfied with their relationship with their mothers. Eighty-four percent rated that relationship on the positive side and 16% said that they were not satisfied. See Table 2.

Table 2. Relationship rating with mother

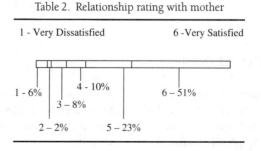

Table 3. Relationship rating with father

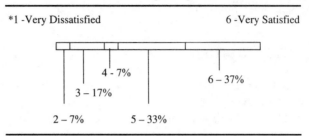

*1 -Very Dissatisfied   6 -Very Satisfied

4 - 7%

3 – 17%

6 – 37%

2 – 7%   5 – 33%

*(On a scale from 1 to 6, scale point 1 was not endorsed by any subject.)

Only 45% of our subjects' fathers were living. The age of those fathers ranged from 70 to 84. Ninety-three percent of them were healthy. One was in a nursing home and one was being taken care of by a family member. (See Figures 23 and 24.)

Ten percent of our subjects said that they had daily contact with their fathers. Fifty-three percent contact their fathers weekly, and 37% contact their fathers monthly or less. None of the men had no contact with his father. (See Figure 25.)

Thirty-seven percent of our subjects said that they were very satisfied with their relationship with their father. Altogether 77% rated that relationship on the positive side and 24% stated that they were not satisfied with that relationship. See Table 3.

Studies indicate how people recall their childhood is to some extent a function of how they feel now. The fact that the great majority of our subjects recalled their relationship with their parents when they were adolescents in a positive way may reflect positively on their current feelings toward their parents. (See Figures 26 and 27.)

In short, the men we studied are close to their parents, like them, and are satisfied with their relationship. The majority of our subjects have never felt alienated from their parents, or held a grudge against them. Instead their parents have served as models for them, as to how to live their lives. Our subjects see themselves as following in their parents' footsteps.

THE SUBJECTS' SIBLINGS

Twelve percent of our subjects were only children. Thirty-seven percent had one sibling; 31% had two siblings; 10% had three; and 8% had four or more. Five of our subjects' siblings (or 4%) died during the past twenty-five years, when they were between the ages of 37 and 52. (See Figure 28.)

The age of the living sibs ranged from 34 to 57. As might be expected, there were almost an equal number of brothers and sisters. When we asked our subjects how emotionally close they are to their siblings, about half said they are close. (See Figures 29 and 30.)

These men feel a little closer to their brothers than to their sisters. Thirty-eight percent of the subjects feel close or very close to their male siblings, compared to 27% who feel that close to their female siblings. Thirty-nine percent of the subjects felt moderately close to their male siblings as compared to 38% of their female siblings. At the negative extreme, they were similar: they were not close to 19% of both their male and female siblings. (See Figures 31 and 32.)

The relationship between siblings contrasts with that between these men and their parents. We do not think it had anything to do with how close they lived geographically. Some siblings just do not like one another. Whether this dislike is a continuation of sibling rivalry from childhood we do not know. But it surprised us that in the middle of the good relationship between parents and children, there would be such variation in the relationship with siblings. At least from our limited data set, we saw great variability in how much our subjects liked their siblings. They liked their male siblings somewhat more.

We should really not be that surprised by our findings. One of the oldest and most fascinating stories about siblings and their relationships is the story of Joseph from the Bible. The siblings could not wait to get rid of Joseph and sold him as a slave. The story does have a happy ending though, as Joseph saves his brothers from starvation.

MARRIED LIFE

Sixty-nine percent of our subjects were married at the time of the interview. Nine percent were living with a partner of the opposite sex. None were living with a partner of the same sex. Nineteen percent were divorced and not remarried or separated. Five percent never had married. One man never married and was living alone. One was widowed. (See Figure 33.)

Of those who ever had been married, 78% had been married only once. Only one man had been married as many as 3 times. Seventy-eight percent of those who are currently married are married to the woman they originally married. Of the total group, 42% had been divorced at some time. (See Figures 34, 35, and 36.)

The great majority of our married subjects were happy with their marriages. On the scale of 1 to 6, most of our subjects, 89%, rated their marriages as satisfying or very satisfying. Only 4% rated their marriages as not satisfying. None rated their marriage as very dissatisfying. See Table 4. This demonstrates that on the whole our subjects are pleased with their marriages, are proud to be married, and enjoy their relationship with their spouses.

Table 4. Subject's Marital Satisfaction

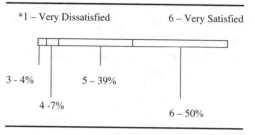

*1 – Very Dissatisfied   6 – Very Satisfied

3 - 4%   5 – 39%

4 -7%

6 – 50%

*(On a scale from 1 to 6, scale points 1 and 2 was not endorsed by any subject.)

Ninety-one percent of the couples combined their incomes. Eighty-seven percent made financial decisions with their wives. Every married subject said he and his wife made major decisions together.

We were interested in finding out how the subjects and their wives divided chores in the home. What is the division of labor? Is it equal between husband and wife? Or does the division of labor resound along more traditional lines?

For the most part, at least in our group, tradition prevails. In 76% of the marriages, the wife does most or all of the cooking. The husband does most or all of the cooking in only 9% of the families. For half the couples, the wife is the primary dishwasher; the husband does them primarily in 17% of the cases; they share in dishwashing in 28% of the cases. For 76% of the couples, the wife does most of the laundry. Forty-six percent of the husbands do the lawn maintenance; a service does the lawn maintenance in 26% of the cases. For 61% of the couples, the wife does most of the grocery shopping; 28% of the couples share this responsibility. Fifty-nine percent of the wives do most or all of the house cleaning; a service does the house cleaning for 22% of the couples. (See Figures 37, 38, 39, 40, 41, and 42.)

On the whole, the group of wives was healthy (83%). The 8 wives who were not healthy suffered from these physical or mental problems: asthma; depression; chronic fatigue; history of heart attack; low blood count; multiple sclerosis; gall bladder problems; and black lung disease (silicosis).

When asked how they met their wives, 26% of the subjects said they met at work, 20% met in college, 17% met at social events, 13% were fixed up in a "blind date," and 9% were friends from high school.

A little over half or 57% lived with their wives before they married. When asked if living together was different than being married, 75% of those who had lived together said, "No."

Altogether our subjects depicted their relationship with their wives very much as that between husband and the old fashioned housewife of years ago. There is no question that there is more variability and change in the role of women, but it has not greatly affected our group.

THE UNMARRIED MENS' RELATIONSHIP WITH WOMEN

In this section, we will describe the men who are widowed, divorced, separated or living with a partner. In addition, we will discuss the one subject who never married and was living alone.

Those men who are separated reported causes of the separation as including disagreements about money and affairs by the husband or wife. They also cited no longer having been in love with their wife, or simply not wanting to be married any longer.

When the seven individuals who were currently divorced and living alone were asked why they got divorced, two cited money issues, one an affair, two being no longer in love, one lack of sex, and one cited "other reasons."

The one individual who never married and was living alone said that he would like to have a relationship but would not want to get married. He is a very shy individual who said he would like a girlfriend but does not want a legal bond.

The one widowed man had lost his wife from breast cancer one month before his interview. He was very cooperative but recalling his spouse was a painful experience for him. They had had a very good relationship, had been partners in their marriage, and he was deeply grieving for her, he said.

RELATIONSHIPS WITH CHILDREN

Seventy-three percent of our subjects had children. See Table 5. Eight-three percent of those who did not have children, made a personal choice not to have any. For 17%, there was no choice: they or their wives biologically could not have children. Those who had children had a total of 113, of whom 57% were girls and 43% were boys or an average of 1.69 children per subject. Obviously, having at least 2 children per man is the mathematical minimum for perpetuating a group. Most fathers (59%) had 2 children; 22% had 3; 8% had 4 or 5 children; 10% had 1 child. (See Figures 43, 44, and 45.)

Table 5. Whether has a child

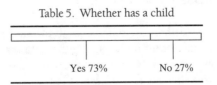

Yes 73%   No 27%

Table 6. Like being a parent

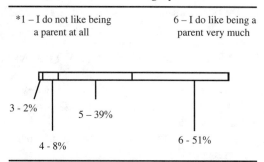

*1 – I do not like being   6 – I do like being a
   a parent at all   parent very much

3 - 2%

5 – 39%

4 - 8%

6 - 51%

*(On a scale from 1 to 6, scale point 1 and 2 was not endorsed by any subject)

When asked to rate relationships with their children, the great majority of the fathers, 76%, rated them (5) or (6) or good or very good. Only 13% rated the relationship as poor. (See Figure 46.) Ninety percent reported greatly liking to be a parent; only 2% did not like being a parent. See Table 6.

Our subjects' relationship with their male children was a little better than their relationship with their daughters. Forty-nine percent rated the relationship with their sons as excellent as compared to an excellent relationship with only 30% of their daughters. Six percent of the fathers rated their relationship with their daughters as very poor. No father rated his relationship with his son as very poor. Their relationship with their older children (beyond high school age) was more polarized than that with their younger children (through high school age). Forty-two percent of the fathers felt their relationship with their older children as excellent, but only 34% noted their relationship with their younger children that favorably. On the other hand, 14% of the fathers viewed their relationship with their older children negatively; only 8% of the fathers viewed their relationship with their younger children that way. (See Figures 47, 48, 49, and 50.)

Altogether, these men enjoyed their children and deeply valued their relationship with them. That relationship persisted into their children's adulthood.

THE FAMILY ACROSS GENERATIONS[1]

The data showed that there are differences in the subjects' family life at age 48 related to the three adolescent routes. Using the statistical method of Analysis of Variance (Anova), we compared the percentage of the Continuous, Surgent, and Tumultuous Groups (see Chapter 3) with respect to the percent of each group who

Table 7. Percent Married

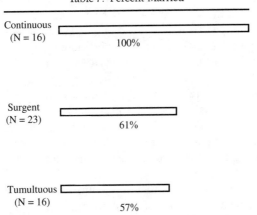

Continuous
(N = 16)
100%

Surgent
(N = 23)
61%

Tumultuous
(N = 16)
57%

are currently married. We also compared the groups with respect to being married and never divorced. Relationships were considered significant if they were at the .05 level or less.

One finding was that the Continuous Group is far more likely than the other groups to be married and to be married to the same person initially married. See Table 7.

Ninety-four percent of the Continuous Group are married and never were divorced as opposed to 43% and 38% respectively of the Surgent and Tumultuous Groups (see Figure 51).

Further analyses of variance were conducted with the three routes as the independent variable and four variables, described below, serving as the dependent variables. Our prediction was that the Continuous Group would be more traditional in their family relations and roles than the other two groups. We further predicted that the Tumultuous Group would be the least traditional in their family relations and roles.

The first variable formed was called "Traditional Family." This variable consists of the following sub-variables:

1. Whether currently married
2. Whether has been divorced
3. Whether spends leisure time available with his family
4. Whether wife does most or all of the cooking

The score was higher if the person is currently married and never was divorced; if the wife does most or all of the cooking; and if the subject spends most of his leisure time with his family. We tested the internal consistency of this variable through the use of alpha (Cronbach & Glaser, 1965). The alpha for the Traditional Family variable was .81. The Continuous Group had the highest Traditional Family score. They are significantly more likely to be married and to be involved in traditional family relationships. (See Figure 52.)

We conducted further analyses using t-tests comparing the Continuous and Tumultuous groups with respect to other variables. The results show that the Continuous Group attends religious services significantly more often than does the Tumultuous Group. (See Figure 53.) Moreover, the Tumultuous Group reported taking significantly more leisure time each week, while the Continuous Group attested to engaging in more frequent exercise than did the Tumultuous Group. (See Figures 54 and 55.)

In summary, our findings are that the Continuous Group subjects, the most healthy, are most likely to be currently married and never to have been divorced. They also are most likely to go to church, exercise, and spend what leisure time they do take with their family.

Conversely, the Tumultuous Group, the least healthy, are least likely to be married, go to church, or exercise. They are most likely to engage in long hours of leisure time activity.

The teenagers who most successfully and smoothly coped with adolescence, the Continuous Group continued to live lives in harmony with their background. Early data had shown that these teenagers tended to have positive family experiences. As teenagers, they tended to reflect their family's values. As adults, they continue to live their lives in this manner, expressing, validating, endorsing, and living out traditional family roles, and relationships. The Continuous Growth Group, our early research showed, had little to no adolescent turmoil and sailed through adolescence and young adulthood. Twenty-seven years later this group in some ways still stands out from the other two developmental groups. They have more traditional families and interests, mirroring the families of their childhood and adolescence.

The Tumultuous Group, by contrast, was more likely to come from disrupted or disturbing backgrounds, to be disturbed as teenagers, and to be less focused on family and traditional institutions as adults.

The Surgent Group was between these two poles, less well-adjusted than the Continuous Group but better adjusted than the Tumultuous Group in adolescence while continuing this pattern into their middle-age years.

PHYSICAL HEALTH

The group as a whole was physically healthy. One suffered from back problems sustained in an accident in his home. Another had diabetes. Others suffered from the following problems to a minor degree: arthritis, migraine headaches, high

Table 8. Weight

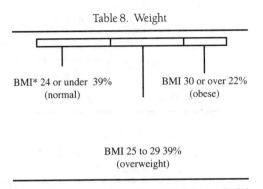

BMI* 24 or under 39%   BMI 30 or over 22%
        (normal)   (obese)

BMI 25 to 29 39%
(overweight)

*BMI = Body Mass Index is defined as weight in kilograms divided
by height in meters squared.

cholesterol, and hypertension. The problem that was most prevalent in our group was being overweight or being obese. See Table 8. Thirty-nine of our subjects had normal weight. Another thirty-nine percent were overweight, and twenty-two percent were obese.

Subjects were asked whether they exercise and 70% said they do. (See Figure 56.) Of these subjects, 32% exercise daily; 45% exercise two to three times a week; 21% weekly; and 2% occasionally. (See Figure 57.)

Twenty one percent of our subjects currently smoke cigarettes. Eighty-six percent of those who smoke, smoke more than a pack a day. Seven percent smoke 10 to 19 cigarettes per day, and 7% smoke occasionally. Of the 79% of the subjects who do not smoke, 55% smoked in the past, but quit. (See Figures 58, 59, and 60.) Most of them stopped smoking years ago, the majority quitting in their 20's.

MENTAL HEALTH

There were relatively few mental illnesses. No one had Schizophrenia or psychosis. No one was severely depressed or suicidal. As can be seen in the responses to the SCL-90 (see Appendix D), the group as a whole was symptom free and quite healthy.

The vast majority of symptoms were not endorsed or endorsed only to a slight degree by this group. There are some symptoms that about a quarter of the group endorsed to a moderate degree. These symptoms included feeling critical of others, feeling irritable, having low energy, and feeling blocked in getting things done. In other words, about a quarter of the group experienced symptoms of mild to moderate stress. None attested to severe symptoms such as hearing voices.

The one area that our subjects did have a problem with was substance abuse. Seven percent are relatively frequent users of marijuana, using marijuana at least

Table 9. Currently drink alcohol

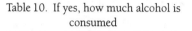

	Yes	No	No answer
	67%	31%	1%

Table 10. If yes, how much alcohol is
consumed

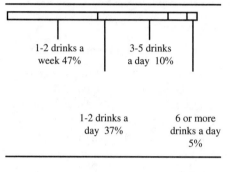

1-2 drinks a week 47%	3-5 drinks a day 10%
1-2 drinks a day 37%	6 or more drinks a day 5%

once a week. Another 45% were not using marijuana but had smoked marijuana in the past. (See Figures 61 and 62.) One subject is currently using cocaine. Nineteen percent had used cocaine in the past and had quit doing so. No one had ever used heroin.

Our subjects had problems with the use of alcohol.
Two thirds of the subjects currently drink alcohol. See Table 9. As can be seen, the amount of alcohol consumed varies considerably. See Table 10.

Ten percent of the group attest to consuming 3 to 5 drinks a day, which is suggestive of problems with alcohol. Another 5% reported having 6 or more drinks a day, which is indicative of alcohol abuse.

Only 3% had drank heavily in the past but were able to stop. Thirteen percent stated that they have or had a problem with alcohol. In contrast, 7% reported never having drunk alcohol.

SEXUALITY

The kind of life a man leads, the family he has, his work, and his leisure activities are set by the time he reaches the age of 48. Sex is no exception.

Table 11. Sexual Satisfaction with Current Sex
Life Rating

1 - Very Dissatisfied	6 -Very Satisfied

1 - 1%	3 – 9%	5 – 28%

2 – 7%	4 - 28%	6 – 25%

While the object of a person's sexuality clearly is highly varied, our subjects' sexuality was uniform in one respect. Not one endorsed having a homosexual or bisexual orientation. Not every subject was sexually active. Seventy-nine percent were while 21% were not. (See Figure 63.)

The frequency of their sexual activity is highly varied. The majority (52%) attested to having sex 2 to 4 times a month. Eighteen percent report having no sex or sex only once or twice a year. Thirty percent report having sex twice a week or more. (See Figure 64.)

Married men's sexual activity is very different from that of the group as a whole. Only 4% report having had no sex or sex only once or twice a year. Seventy-two percent report having sex 2 to 4 times a month. Only 23% attest to having sex twice a week or more in contrast to the 30% for the group as a whole. (See Figure 65.)

As Table #11 shows, 17% of the entire group of men said they were dissatisfied with their sex life. Of the 81% who are satisfied, approximately equal proportions were somewhat satisfied, satisfied, and very satisfied.

Our data show the number of partners that our subjects had in their lifetime. Twelve percent reported having had only one partner. Thirty-three percent had between two to four partners. The majority had between 2 and 10 partners. Thirty-one percent had between 11 and 99 partners. Two of the men reported having had over 100 partners. (See Figure 66.)

Almost the same percent (17% vs. 18%) of the total group and the part of that group who are married report being dissatisfied with their current sex life. The percentage of each group who are quite or very satisfied is almost identical as well (53% versus 57%), with the married men being slightly higher. (See Figure 67.)

Fewer men (22%) attested to having had romantic relationships outside marriage than did those who reported having had sex outside marriage. (See Figure 68.) Of the subjects who are or have been married, 30% reported having had sex outside of their marriage. (See Figure 69.)

MEMORY[2]—REALITY OR MYTH

This section compares responses given by subjects when they were in high school and at age 48. When they were 14 years old, subjects were asked about their current family relationships, home environment, dating, sexuality, religion, type of discipline received, and activities. At age 48, they were asked to respond to the same questions concerning how they believed they felt when they were in high school.

To make sure our subjects understood exactly what was being asked of them, eight questions about their experiences in high school were asked in two different ways. First they were asked about an experience or feeling when they were in high school. Then they were asked how they believe they responded when they were in high school when asked about that experience or feeling. For example, first they were asked what they recalled their father's worst trait was during their high school years. Then they were asked how they thought they would have answered the same question during their high school years. Analyses showed no difference in the pattern of responses to these two ways of asking seven of these questions. With respect to the eighth question, "When in high school, did girls like you?" When asked in the form, "Did girls like you?" 82% of the subjects said, "Yes." When asked in the form, "How would you have answered that when you were in high school?" 61% said, "Yes." To focus subjects on how they would have responded then versus what they believed now, questions often were asked in the form, "When you were in high school, did you etc.?" Consequently, results will be presented as reflecting how subjects recalled their adolescence versus how in fact they experienced it during that stage of their lives.

Results of comparisons between responses given when the subjects were in high school and at age 48 are shown in Table 12. These results show marked differences between 48-year-old subjects' recall of how they thought and felt at age 14 and what they thought and felt at age 14.

The data show that we would have a very different picture of the subjects' adolescence if we based our impressions on what they said during their teenage years as opposed to reports they gave as adults.

To illustrate, 28% of the teenage boys said that they did not like high school and homework. During adulthood, however, 58% of the subjects recalled not liking school and homework. Eighty-two percent of the boys reported that they were disciplined through the use of physical punishment, whereas only 33% as men stated that they had received such punishment. Clearly, there were significant discrepancies between reports as adolescents and later recall of their adolescence as adults.

Other examples include: 30% of subjects recalled at age 48 that they were their mother's favorite, whereas only 14% said that when they were in high school, they were their mother's favorite. Significantly, the percentage of the subjects who saw themselves as having been their mother's favorite doubled at age 48. When they were in high school, 48% saw their father's best trait as being emotionally

Table 12. Percent endorsement of items when subjects were in high school and at age 48 regarding high school experiences or attitudes

	Percent Endorsement	
	When in high school	Age 48
Family Relationships		
1. What is (was) your mother's best trait?		
Competence	27	28
Relationship with subject	17	39
Intelligence and knowledge	3	3
Discipline	5	0
Emotionally responsive	48	30
2. What is (was) your father's best trait?		
Competence	23	33
Relationship with subject	21	25
Intelligence and knowledge	7	11
Discipline	1	1
Emotionally responsive	48	30
3. What is (was) your mother's worst trait?		
Impulsivity	32	17
Non-affectional (does not show feelings)	24	2
Incompetent and unintelligent	2	11
Relations with subject	14	23
Discipline	9	19
Habits	19	28
4. What is (was) your father's worst trait?		
Impulsivity	41	26
Non-affectional (does not show feelings)	27	11
Incompetent and unintelligent	4	2
Relations with subject	7	21
Discipline	7	12
Habits	14	28
5. Who is (was) your mother's favorite?		
I was	14	30
Another sibling	86	70
6. Who is (was) your father's favorite?		
I was	28	26
Another sibling	72	74
7. Which parent do (did) you take after?		
Father	71	49
Mother	29	51
8. Do (Did) you expect to earn more money than your father?		
Yes	70	65
No	30	35
Home Environment		
9. What is (was) the nicest thing about your home life?		
Physical comfort	9	19

(*Continued*)

Table 12. (*Continued*)

	Percent Endorsement	
	When in high school	Age 48
Emotional Comfort	61	55
Closeness with parents	21	23
Other responses	9	3
10. What is (was) the worst thing about your home life?		
Physical comfort	40	15
Emotional Comfort	11	50
Overt Family conflict	13	33
Sibling Rivalry	16	2
Decrease in self-esteem	20	0
11. What would you like (have liked) to change in your home life?		
Physical setting	27	14
Emotional environment	12	33
Relationship with parents	19	24
Relationship with siblings	13	6
Dependence—independence	7	6
Nothing	22	17
12. Do (Did) your parents work on projects together?		
Yes	66	36
No	34	64
13. Which one of your parents makes (made) most of the decisions?		
Father	76	55
Mother	24	45
Dating and Sexuality		
14. Do (Did) girls like you?		
Yes	98	86
No	2	14
15. Is (was) it important for you to have a girlfriend?		
Yes	62	61
No	38	39
16. Is (was) it easy for you to get a date?		
Yes	77	65
No	23	35
17. When is (was) sexual intercourse O.K.?		
Anytime during high school	15	44
After high school	32	23
Only for married people	53	33
Religion		
18. Is (was) religion helpful to you?		
Yes	70	26
No	30	74

(*Continued*)

Table 12. (*Continued*)

	Percent Endorsement	
	When in high school	Age 48
Discipline		
19. Describe the discipline you receive(d) from your mother.		
Strict	36	30
Not Strict	64	70
20. Describe the discipline you receive(d) from your father.		
Strict	21	48
Not Strict	79	52
21. Is (was) the discipline you receive(d) consistent?		
Yes	49	17
No	51	83
22. Is (was) the discipline you receive(d) upsetting to you?		
Yes	12	49
No	88	51
23. Is (was) the discipline you receive(d) unfair?		
Yes	12	22
No	88	78
24. Do (Did) you receive physical punishment as discipline?		
Yes	82	33
No	18	67
25. Is (Was) love withheld as punishment?		
Yes	8	14
No	92	86
Activities		
26. What do (did) you enjoy most?		
Physical outlets	61	23
Relationships with peers	24	52
Mental activities	5	23
Family relationships	10	2
27. What do (did) you enjoy least?		
Physical work	19	6
School and homework	28	58
Peer relationships	18	24
Other	35	12
28. Do (Did) your parents encourage you to be active in sports?		
Yes	60	38
No	40	62

responsive. This dropped to 30% at age 48. Instead at age 48, 33% saw their father's best trait as competency.

When in high school, it was much more likely that they saw themselves as taking after their father (71%) than they believed was true at age 48 (49%). As teenagers, three quarters of the subjects identified their father as the parent who made most of the decisions. That percentage fell to 55% at age 48. They were much more likely at age 48 to see their mother as having had decision-making power than they were in high school.

When in high school, the subjects were much more likely to perceive that girls liked them and that it was easy for them to get a date than was true of their recall of their perceptions at age 48. Their recall at age 48 of themselves as teenagers reflects less confidence in their ability to be liked by the opposite sex than was true of their perceptions of themselves as teenagers.

The adults recall themselves as being much more liberal sexually than they actually were when they were teenagers. Fifty-three percent of the subjects when in high school said that sexual intercourse is only for married people, which was by far the most endorsed category. At age 48, they tended to recall believing as teenager that sex was okay anytime during high school (44%).

Seventy percent of the subjects at age 14 cited religion as being helpful to them. At age 48, 74% of the subjects stated that they did not feel that religion was helpful to them as teenagers. These statistics reflect a dramatic difference in perspectives as to the role of religion in the lives of these subjects in high school.

As we will discuss more fully later, these data call into question the accuracy of adults' memory of their adolescence. In their prior work, the two senior authors showed that there was essentially no correlation between subjects' recall of how they felt and thought as teenagers and how in fact they did feel and think at that age. Here we take this finding one step further. Not only did our subjects not recall their adolescence accurately, they tended to recall their experience as being more like a stereotype of adolescence than in fact was the case. This finding, we will point out, has implications for understanding human memory as well as the developmental process of becoming a mature adult.

NOTES

1. Published, in part, in "Continuity of Family Constellation" by Offer, D., Kaiz, M., Ostrov, E., and Albert, D.B., in *Adolescent & Family Health*, vol 3, #1, p. 3–8, 2003.
2. Based on "The Altering of Reported Experiences" by Offer, Kaiz, Howard, and Bennett, *J. Am. Acad. Child and Adolesc. Psychiatry*, 39:6, June 2000, p:735–742.

Chapter 7

Tony, Bob, and Carl In Late Adulthood[1]

We last saw Tony, Bob, and Carl in 1971 as they were heading into the wider world. Each represented a different style of growth through adolescence and young adulthood. Tony was an illustration of Continuous development; Bob exemplified the Surgent route; and Carl was a sample of the Tumultuous path. As was true about all the men, when we interviewed them in 1996, we were highly curious as to how their lives evolved.

TONY

Tony, as we saw, was the exemplification of the Continuous Group. Handsome, athletic, academically accomplished, Tony sailed through adolescence, capitalizing on opportunities, unmarred by their risks. Tony demonstrated clearly a major finding of Offer & Offer (1975) and subsequent works, that adolescence need not be a time of turmoil, rebellion, and angst. Tony too is the kind of person whose future others might wonder about. Would he continue his smooth course? Or would his ship be wrecked against the shoals of real life as he moves away from the harbor of his parents home or college? The course he did take follows.

At first, life after college proceeded much as expected for handsome, perpetually successful Tony Canfield. At age 26, he was living in Michigan, in his third year of the rigorous J.D./PhD. program in forensic psychology that he had begun immediately after college graduation. That year, he also married his college girlfriend, Rhonda, who had moved with him to Michigan. The couple had been

71

living together happily for three years, and marriage didn't immediately change that: "Marriage wasn't terribly different from living together," Tony said, "I was busy and all that, but I didn't let it interfere with Rhonda coming first."

Tony's mother, who had initially opposed the marriage on the grounds that it could derail her son's career plans, had nothing to fear. To the contrary, Tony worked even harder in his last four years of graduate school. He passed the Michigan state bar and won an elite fellowship that bolstered his already-impressive resume. In the meantime, money was tight for the newlyweds. They lived in a small apartment that was an easy commute to Tony's workplace, and Rhonda worked as a secretary.

But as Tony settled in Michigan, the secure network of the close-knit Canfield family began to unravel. His brother, Jim, with whom he had been extremely close, joined a law firm in Western Illinois, a four-hour drive from the family home in the suburbs of Chicago. His sister, Carol, moved to the East Coast to attend college, and she and Tony spoke infrequently. "When I really started my career, I wouldn't call my siblings for months at a time," Tony admitted, "Jim was married and had a son, I was so preoccupied, he was so preoccupied . . . I feel bad that we didn't spend more time together."

On the other hand, Tony's emotional relationship to both his parents became stronger after college. He had often argued with his mother over the issue of whether or not a serious relationship with a woman would come between him and his career, but his marriage to Rhonda diffused that worry, and other old conflicts seemed to fade away as well. "As the years went by, my mother mellowed," Tony said. Tony also realized that his father wasn't as judgmental about his achievements as he had previously thought. "My dad never really put pressure on us, I just felt that I wanted to please him," he said. And yet, his warm feelings for his parents did not cause Tony to make an effort to spend time with them. "I was always too busy," he admitted.

In 1980, Tony was offered a job with the state of Michigan that secured his professional future. He worked with a group of prosecutors, and his job was to determine whether clients were mentally fit to stand trial. The hours were lengthy—ten to twelve hour days—and the work was extremely stressful. Many of the clients were facing the death penalty, so Tony was forced to listen to grueling murder cases and watch grieving families celebrate or suffer under his ruling. Ever ambitious, Tony was determined not to show any emotion, no matter how painful the case. "I always thought I was this big tough person who could handle very traumatic cases . . . I did very well with it and people would congratulate me. They couldn't believe I was handling major cases like this."

After so many years of school, it was a relief for Tony to feel he was being well compensated for the work he had trained so hard to do. "I think I caught a wave of interest in my profession," he acknowledged. He and Rhonda moved into a small house in one of the nicest neighborhoods in the area, and Rhonda quit her job to take care of the house full time. And yet, in this seemingly happy time, their marriage had begun to show signs of strain. "As I got more involved in my career, we spent less time together," said Tony. "She had her set of friends, I was at the office. I just couldn't juggle my schedule to fit her in anymore. It wasn't working out." Ever shy of confrontation, Tony refused to admit to himself that his work habits were the cause of the trouble. "We never faced the issue that time together was the problem," he later admitted.

When his marriage with Rhonda hit an impasse, Tony decided to find his own apartment. During this time, he began seeing a co-worker, Melanie. "It was a relationship of convenience," he said, "We were both lawyers and we were both living at the office all the time." The relationship perfectly suited his needs at the time. "It was sort of a whirlwind sexual convenient relationship, but not a committed relationship," he said.

After six months of living on his own, however, Tony felt the pull of his comfortable home life with Rhonda. Plus, his relationship with Melanie had cooled. "I realized it was an impossible situation, our personalities and goals were different, it was something that would never work out," he said. The relationship ended with little drama. "We went our own ways and it was mutual, no one was crushed or anything," he said. Tony moved back in with Rhonda, and for a time, tried to alter his schedule to spend more time with his wife. They embarked on a major home renovation project, adding several more rooms to the house. Yet Tony quickly found himself slipping back into his old habits: "I was trying to make more of an effort, but my behavior problem was still the same," he said later.

In 1983, Tony made a decision that would make his already-grueling schedule even tougher. Despite the prestige of his government position, Tony had known for some time that he could make far more money developing a private practice. The trade-off, of course, was that developing a successful business would mean working even longer hours. But when one of his colleagues broached the idea of joining a successful partnership owned by two attorneys who were nearing retirement age, Tony could not resist. "It was a good basis to start and then we could keep the ball rolling," he said. But his workdays did lengthen, from twelve hours to fourteen—or more—and he worked every weekend as well.

Tony was surprised that the business took off so quickly. "The number of clients I have, how busy I am, has even surpassed what I expected to do, the economics have surpassed what I expected to achieve," he remarked. His work could also be immensely fulfilling: "When I have a client come in and I am able to make a difference in their lives, I feel a great deal of satisfaction, I truly enjoy it," he said. Yet his level of stress had also increased exponentially.

Sometimes, his firm represented clients involved in high-profile lawsuits that were well reported in the press; more frequently, Tony's cases involved violent crimes such as murder or rape. As an expert witness, Tony had to carefully read through police and autopsy reports detailing some of the most horrific, gruesome crimes imaginable. One of his clients had repeatedly raped his young daughter;

another had bludgeoned his elderly grandmother to death with a metal pipe because she had refused to give him money for a videogame. Tony often had intense feelings about his cases, but felt it was extremely important not to let his clients or his office peers know what his feelings were. "In terms of family, my relationships and my marriage, my work has taken a big toll," he admitted. "I had to cut off my emotions." The endless work weeks—often 80 to 100 hours—only added to his stress level.

Throughout college and in his first years of work, Tony had developed the habit of pouring himself a drink or two to help him relax after work. But as the daily job pressures mounted, he found that he needed more alcohol to render himself emotionally numb. A drink or two turned into four or five, and soon, Tony was drunk in the evening more often than not. But he saw no similarities between himself and other people he had known to have drug or alcohol problems. "I was never one of those people in the sixties who just wanted to get completely ripped or drop out of life," he said. "I would just pour myself a few drinks, just take enough so I could . . . drop feelings." Tony believed that as long as he was at his desk each morning, the daily alcohol dose was simply what was necessary for him to maintain his calm, professional veneer. "I just didn't want to feel . . . I was dealing with a lot of suffering and I was more sensitive than I realized," he said. "If I just send some poor guy to prison for life, or to his death, I wanted to go home and cry, but I couldn't do that—I always had to look good on the outside. So I would just stuff it."

In 1985, Tony's mother Joanne was diagnosed with cancer and died six months later. "Before she died, I was just starting to feel really close to her, there was much less of a barrier between us," he said. Faced with a personal tragedy, Tony immediately turned to the coping methods that functioned so well for him in his day-to-day life. "I just stuffed it like I was doing with everything else in my life," he said, "I was in the middle of developing a successful business. The day she died, I was in the middle of an important case, I flew to Chicago and buried her and flew back and was in the courtroom the next day." Tony was impressed that his father, who had never shown much emotion during his childhood, was able to express a great deal of sadness over his mother's illness. "I saw how my dad was capable of taking care of my mother when she was sick, and he went through all the emotions, survived and went on," Tony said, "I always felt if you showed that kind of emotion you would self-destruct, you couldn't function."

Joanne Canfield's death did little to mend the frayed relationship between Tony and his siblings. Later that year, his brother, Jim checked himself into the Hazelton Clinic, admitting that he had an alcohol problem that was spinning out of control. Though Jim was unaware of the extent to which Tony had also become dependent on alcohol, he nevertheless called Tony to remind him that substance abuse often stems from a genetic disposition. "Jim called me from the clinic and told me I should watch myself, but I thought, I am too successful, I have a booming legal practice, one of the best practices of its kind in the area," Tony said.

Jim joined AA and continued to remain sober. At a family gathering the following year, Tony noticed that Jim was once again becoming close with their father and even their sister, Carol, who had permanently settled on the East Coast and had a family of her own. Tony, on the other hand, was even more emotionally withdrawn from his clan. He had fallen back into his workaholic patterns, and his daily drinking habit had increased to at least six drinks every night. But Tony saw no connection between his drinking and the distance between himself and his family; rather, he had convinced himself that his drinking habits were within the acceptable limits of normal behavior. "I felt that I had a habit and Jim had a problem," he said, "I was in total denial."

Throughout the next eight years, Tony's life was a blur of work, alcohol, and more work. As the time slipped by, it became apparent that he and Rhonda were not going to have children. "It was sort of an unconscious choice by both of us, we knew that when I went into business for myself I would be living at the office much of the time, and we didn't want to bring children into that environment," he said, "We never sat down and said we weren't going to have children, but before we knew it I was in my forties and Rhonda was in her late thirties." Although Tony and Rhonda appeared every inch the happy couple, Tony's alcohol use had, in fact, nearly suffocated the emotional connection between them. "I am a provider, but as far as emotional and moral support, I haven't been there for Rhonda," he admitted, "My behavior has forced her to become rather hard at times and sometimes it rubs me the wrong way." Their sex life suffered as well. At the same time, Tony relied on his wife to take care of everything related to their home life, including bill payments and investing decisions. In those matters, he trusted Rhonda completely. "If we have a major decision Rhonda will sit down and present things, she is very good at getting information," he said, "I can't think of a single time she has misled me."

Not surprisingly, the people in Tony's life to whom he felt closest to were his co-workers. "Sometimes I see my partners more than my wife, you get very close sharing difficult cases and difficult experiences. The professional bond breaks down into a personal bond." His friends outside of work, he admitted, were largely Rhonda's. "She has spent much more time cultivating friendships, and she is very good at it," he said ruefully.

Then, in 1993, Tony's hidden life exploded. Suddenly, he found that drinking no longer seemed to have the same calming effect. "I couldn't figure out what was happening to me," Tony said later, "Why I was feeling anxious about my marriage, anxious about my work . . . the feelings came through the drink and I had panic attacks, I was depressed and anxious." Tony knew that the easiest way to quell his anxiety would be to drink more. But to do so would mean drinking during working hours, which would cross the boundary he had long ago drawn for himself between habitual drinker and serious alcoholic. "Always in the back of my mind I knew that what I was doing was wrong," he said, "But I thought I needed the alcohol to continue my work. Then all of a sudden they weren't working for me."

Tony knew it was time for him to face the harsh reality of his alcoholism. "I realized that if I didn't take a step here, my life was over," he said. Afraid of losing his job and business, he felt that checking into an in-patient rehab program was not an option. In the end, he admitted the problem to only three people: his wife Rhonda, his brother Jim and the co-worker he was closest to, one of the original partners in the firm. He told the rest of his co-workers that he was suffering from exhaustion and needed to take a month off work. Then he quit drinking cold turkey, forcing himself to remain in his living room as he endured a brutal withdrawal sickness. "It was terrible," said Tony, "After a day I thought it was over, and then in two days it came again. I thought I was going to die."

Later, Tony acknowledged that he might not have been able to cope with his alcoholism without the support of his brother Jim. As soon as Tony told Jim he planned to stop drinking, the years of emotional distance between the brothers quickly faded. In the first month of Tony's sobriety, he spoke to his brother as often as twice a day, and they began visiting each other frequently despite Jim's busy schedule. "Jim was a powerful example because he had already been in AA for almost eight years," Tony said, "He was powerful but not preaching, he was just there and he would share his experience and how he dealt with certain problems. I admire him a lot—he has gone through some tough times, very difficult times and I think that says a lot about my brother."

Tony has remained sober since 1993. "I am very scared of alcohol and all substances now, even cold medicine," he said. Yet facing life without alcohol remains a struggle. "For years, I felt like I was typecast as a busy professional lawyer, and every day was just survival, getting through each case, staying one step ahead of my reputation," he said, "Now I am rediscovering and accepting myself and my limitations. I feel like I can be honest with other people."

And Tony is also painfully aware of the damage that the years of alcoholism and emotional withdrawal did to his marriage. "I haven't nurtured Rhonda the way she has nurtured me," he admitted, "She needs someone to nurture her too, if she has a cold to ask how she is feeling and I have just not been there." For the first time, Tony agreed to attend marital counseling sessions. "I am trying to be here more for everyday things and get our sexual relationship back," he said, "I think the ball is in my court to do something about this relationship."

Since becoming sober, Tony has found tremendous satisfaction in renewing his emotional ties to his father, brother, and sister. "If a week goes by and I don't talk to my brother, I miss him," he said. "Alcohol had interfered with our relationship, but now we have become much closer. I lean on him for moral support, we confide in each other." In the past few years, Tony has become closer to his father as well. "I am trying to capitalize on the good relationship I had with my father when I was a teenager," he said. It has been harder for Tony to establish a friendship with his sister Carol; the two had never been close, and she does not share his substance abuse problem. But Tony is pleased that relations between them are no longer strained; "Since I have been off alcohol our visits are more honest and relaxed," he said.

Despite the difficulties of the past few years, Tony has not lost the optimism and self-confidence that has characterized his positive growth pattern. "I feel strangely optimistic about things as I reflect on my life," he remarked, "I am certainly not thrilled about the years of abusing alcohol and I can't go back and redo that, but I do feel good that I have a second chance." He wants to work fewer hours, and plans to retire within the next five to ten years. "I am not sure what I would do, I would like to take some time just to be with Rhonda first," he said, "I feel that life has been pretty good to me and I would like to give some of that back, work with young people, or volunteer."

In his late forties, Tony has a new attitude towards life, one that would have been anathema to his twenty-year-old self. "Now that I am getting older, I find that marriage, friendships, these are things that are more important than professional accomplishments and money," he said. The boy who had worried so much about what his parents and peers thought of him is now far more concerned with how he feels about himself. "I think over the last couple of years I have enjoyed contact with people more than I ever did before," he said, "I have a long way to go, but I am trying."

Tony, our follow-up study showed, did not sail totally unencumbered and worry free through his twenties and into middle age. He had to work through some significant challenges. He experienced a downward spiral associated with his use of alcohol to cope. But in the end, he was able to transcend the difficulties he faced and achieved a new level of growth and maturity. Thirty-four years after first being studied, Tony continued to function in the psychologically normal, symptom-free range.

BOB

When we left Bob at age 22, he had just graduated from college. In college, he had seemed to founder, trying drugs, changing majors, having a series of unsatisfactory relationships with women. Yet he also had drawn closer to his mother. He seemed eager to put college behind him and find a stable and rewarding position in life, one that would reflect and be compatible with his unique talents and characteristics. His story, spanning ages 23 through 48, follows.

For Bob Rubin, college had been a time of change. As a freshman, he was an introverted, nerdy boy; as a senior, he had become an outspoken, politically conscious man with a large circle of friends. His relationship to his parents had also shifted. In high school, Bob had been quiet and studious; in college, he had openly espoused his radical ideology and sometimes earned poor grades. His parents, Morris and Debra, were hardly thrilled with their son's grades and new political views. "My relationship with both my parents, but especially my father, became estranged for a while," Bob later reflected.

But for all Bob's personal growth during his college years, he continued to struggle with self-confidence issues and was often frustrated in his relationships with women. In his first three years of college he had numerous girlfriends, but none of them proved lasting.

Bob's bachelor days came to an end during his senior year when he met Lori, a beautiful, ambitious Hispanic woman who aspired to be a television news reporter. "What attracted me initially," Bob recalled, "was that she was smart and very sexy. She was a challenge. She was brought up differently, had different ideas and concepts. She represented a different point of view." As was true of several of his previous relationships, Bob's romance with Lori began as a friendship. "We would show up at the same parties and one day just ended up in bed together. Then we started seeing each other semi-regularly."

Although Bob had switched majors several times during college, eventually settling on a double major in Computer Science and Psychology, his career plans seemed well underway by his college graduation. During college, he had interned for two summers at a brokerage firm, and took a job there immediately after school. He continued to date Lori, although the two were not yet making serious plans for the future. "We were very much involved in a strong sexual relationship, but in the early days we thought we would both have jobs and separate apartments and stay best friends probably the rest of our lives," he said.

Nevertheless, Bob's deepening involvement with Lori caused further estrangement from his family. "That Lori was a person of color caused some friction," he said. "Not that my parents were intolerant or unaccepting, but my mother came from a strong family with three older sisters, and I am the youngest of 15 or so cousins who were all getting married, having their homes in suburbia, and doing pretty much what was expected."

Bob felt that his extended family was unable to see beyond their stereotypical image of Hispanics and Hispanic culture. "It is that strange mix of racism and classism that exists among certain suburban Jewish or Protestant families," he noted, "It's not that they dislike people of color because of the color of their skin, it is that they are a different class of people." And yet, when Lori decided to drive to San Francisco after graduation to pursue her journalism career, Debra encouraged Bob to go with her. "My mother said, "Young lady you are not going to drive yourself across country, you have to have somebody help you drive,'" he remembered. "I said I had never been to the West Coast, and so went and spent two weeks there and realized I would much rather live there than Chicago."

Bob had little difficulty finding work in San Francisco. After a month of job-hunting, he landed a position as a programmer for a small research firm. He and Lori found their first house together, and really began to "think of ourselves as a couple," Bob said. Still, they made no move to marry. "It is a strange story in a sense," mused Bob. "We started out as companions and friends and over time we became lovers, but that took a while."

After six years with the research firm, Bob decided to pursue graduate studies in computer engineering at a local university. During his three years as a graduate student, he worked on a variety of freelance jobs, including a stint as a recording engineer. But as always, Bob gravitated back towards work in the technology field; in his final year at the university, he held a position maintaining the university's software library.

Meanwhile, Lori was achieving her own success in television journalism. Bob was thrilled with her accomplishments. "She gets to meet the most interesting people in the world and I get to accompany her," he said. The relationship was also becoming more accepted by Bob's family. "My mother and father accepted Lori after they realized it wasn't just something in passing," he shared. "My aunts and uncles and cousins like to see her on TV, they came to realize she was well known." Still, the couple sometimes faced prejudice, and Bob knew his parents were confused, if not outwardly disapproving, of his choice of both a career and partner. "I think my parents had difficulty explaining what I was doing to people," he said.

In his early thirties, Bob's career took a significant turn. After graduate school, he had joined a firm that specialized in helping commercial clients with their engineering and computer research, rising to a managerial position after four years. From there, he decided to strike out on his own as an independent technical consultant. His nonconformist tendencies, he had realized, were much better suited to the non-corporate life. "I liked the freedom of the work, that I was being paid for my knowledge by the hour and didn't have to be in offices with the same people all the time, doing the same thing all the time," he said.

Happily, Bob discovered that his technical skills were in high demand. His first client, a state government agency that needed upgrades to their computer system, brought him repeated business over the next few years. Next, he created an inventory and tracking system for another early client, a large manufacturing company based in the Midwest, which developed into a decade-long project for a team of consultants. As his consulting projects expanded over the next decade to include a range of small and large clients in various industries, Bob became confident that he would never have to take a full-time job again. The impatience and restlessness that had led him the switch majors three times in college would prove a boon to his consulting career: "I have always had that kind of flexibility and been positioned so that if something fortunate or exciting came along, I could just go for it," he noted.

Starting as a teenager, Bob had always devoted his extra energy to developing interests and personal hobbies. He continued to do so in his thirties, studying languages, (he spoke a smattering of German, French, and Russian), traveling extensively in Africa, and collecting African music. But unlike his teenage self,

Bob discovered in his thirties that he was also a capable athlete who enjoyed windsurfing. "In the mid-eighties, I started enjoying having a body," he said. "I could do things comfortably and gracefully instead of being awkward and nerdy." Physical activity enabled Bob to overcome his former anxieties over his looks. "I developed a pride in my appearance, I'm sort of like one of those guys who gets better looking as they get older," he said.

Still, some of Bob's adolescent social inhibitions persisted into his adult years, causing occasional conflicts in his relationship. "Lori is very social and I was always alone, reading," he said. "I got tired of explaining to people what I did for a living. But she felt I was not as outgoing and sociable as she would have liked me to be." In college, Bob had often turned to drugs as a social lubricant to help him through awkward situations. He continued to use pot and cocaine, sometimes daily, throughout the early 1980's. But as his body image and sense of self-worth improved, he found drugs less compelling. "I have pretty much taken care of that now, although I may smoke a joint once in a while if I have had a hard day at work," he admitted.

As he neared his fortieth birthday, Bob's relationship with his parents shifted yet again. Morris' health declined during the 1980's, and he and Debra retired and moved to a retirement community near Los Angeles. Initially, Bob found visits to his parents' home stressful. "When I went to Los Angeles, it always became a little problematic," he said, "My mother's siblings always compared notes about all of their children and I know my mother felt a little left out." Then, in 1988, his father passed away. Having known his father as an invalid for most of his life, Bob was not as affected by the death as he had thought he might be. "It was sad, it made me a little bit more aware of my own mortality; I miss him, but I don't feel like there is a big void in my life or anything like that," he admitted. What he felt instead was a new perspective on his father and the struggles of their relationship. "In high school, I would have said my dad was boring," he said. "My dad tended to be a little withdrawn, but now I realize it was because he was in pain all the time." And Bob had come to appreciate his father's "easy-going nature" and old world manners. "He never said a bad word about anyone," Bob noted. "He was gentlemanly."

Bob's relationship with his mother also changed after his father's death. Bob arrived in Los Angeles shortly before Morris died, and stayed for a couple of weeks afterwards. During that time, he and Debra worked through many of their old issues, including her feelings about Lori. "We talked and talked," Bob remembered, "I think she understands much about what I did—in fact, she understands completely—and fully understands the choices I have made." Through their hours of conversation, Bob developed a greater insight into his mother's personality, and discovered a new empathy for her. "I have a much better understanding of all the trials and tribulations she lived through, a very, very difficult life," he said, "We are now best friends about everything."

Despite Bob's new appreciation for family life, when he and Lori were in their early forties they made the decision not to start a family of their own. "We had enjoyed talking about it but were never felt we were ready for a family," said Bob, "Then in our forties, we started thinking about it because the clock was running out." As a young man, Bob had envisioned himself with a family, but now felt that he and Lori were happy "being ourselves." Still, he wanted to be sure that Lori would not feel she was missing out. "I asked her if she was just saying okay because it was what I wanted to hear, but finally we were both satisfied that we were comfortable being childless," he said, "And that was it."

Though Bob's work as a freelance programmer came with an unusual amount of autonomy, the nature of the work did require him to move from one lengthy client project to another. But in his mid-forties, he stumbled on a niche that freed him from that constraint. As a longtime computer technician, Bob was an early Internet user, before most people knew what the word meant. In the early 1990's, he developed several websites that became well-known to mainstream computer users. Shortly thereafter, he began teaching and writing articles on Internet technologies. "I found I have a real love for teaching and a real knack for getting up in front of any number of people, be it four or five or three or four hundred," he said. "I like the fact that I am meeting a lot of young people who are very excited about this technology."

Although the hyper-fast pace of his industry occasionally unnerved him ("I always feel like something new is going to come up tomorrow and I am going to miss it," he said), Bob felt that he had finally hit on the career track he had always hoped for. "I always wanted to teach and write and the opportunity came up to do both. I always wanted to not just have a job to have a paycheck, but to do the things that I love." His job and interest now often blended to the point, he noted, where it was hard to distinguish between work and leisure time: "I don't separate my work from my life," he said, "I don't think it is work when I am learning, it is fun. I am sure I work 40 hours a week, I may work more, but I just don't pay attention."

When they reached their mid-forties, Bob and Lori had been unmarried partners for over two decades. Though neither had been entirely faithful throughout their time together the intense fulfillment of their relationship quickly nullified any desire to seek another partner. Lori was Bob's true partner in every sense of the word. "I make all the big decisions and she makes all the important ones," he joked. Bob had entirely bridged the emotional disconnectedness that had prevented him from drawing close to his college girlfriends. Other than occasional concerns about Lori's health—he wished she would lose weight and stop smoking—Bob declared himself "ecstatic" about his relationship. "It just keeps getting better to our own surprise and astonishment," he said, "We love each other tremendously almost to the extent that we start to worry about what is wrong with us."

Though Bob had long been happy with the progress of his career, in his forties he began doing pro bono work for a non-profit organization, which gave him additional satisfaction. Through the organization, Bob went to Peru and helped young students learn about and use Internet technologies. "I get a lot of satisfaction from helping people out," he said, "I knew years and years ago that I wanted to be working more with people. The joy of discovering new things and telling other people about it is the greatest thing in the world."

Now in his late forties, Bob felt at ease with himself and the direction of his life. His unflagging energy was channeled into hobbies and projects he found fascinating; his partnership with Lori was satisfying; he had achieved self-fulfillment in his career without sacrificing the spontaneity and continuous learning that he craved. As a 21 year-old college junior, Bob had been "waiting to get on with my life." As a 47 year-old man, he was content to stay right where he was. "I could look into a crystal ball five years in the future and see what I was doing, it could surprise the hell out of me," he said, "But I know I am on the right track today."

Looking back, it would have been hard to imagine, when Bob was a teenager, the course he wound up taking in life. The insecure, at times floundering, at times rebellious young man became a strong, centered, successful middle-aged man. The marginal young man had become an exemplar of good adjustment.

From the perspective of Bob's parents, he was, at age 14, a somewhat worrisome prospect, like an awkward bird at the edge of the nest, unsure of himself as he was about to embark on that proverbial maiden flight. His parents now would probably breath a sigh of relief. After some hesitation, some swoops and dives, Bob by all measures is doing quite well. He is the embodiment of a principle theme of this book: that with the passage of time, through maturation and life experience, the vagaries and adaptive variations shown among adolescents in the normal range tend to even out. There is a movement to a solid center that, to be sure, allows a wealth of individual variation, but retains as a commonality the self-assurance, fulfillment and connectedness of the normal, well-functioning adult.

CARL

Of the three young men we have highlighted in this book, Carl was the one who experienced the most turmoil as he went through and beyond adolescence. He grew up in a conflictual home with a disturbed and abusive mother and possibly alcoholic father. Consequences for him seemed to include a degree of apathy toward school and lack of self-confidence. Yet he also had considerable resources including sociability, use of humor and pragmatism. At age 22, he seemed to be drifting, unsure where to go. We pick up on his story at age 23.

Though the U.S. was in the midst of the Vietnam War when Carl Benson was drafted, he was lucky enough to avoid active combat. "I had a fear of dying," he said, "I knew guys that died, guys that came back without arms and legs. I didn't want to do that," he said. Despite a lack of a technical background, Carl was able to secure a position as an equipment repairman, helping to maintain communications equipment such as radio receivers. He was stationed at Army bases in Alaska and Hawaii for the duration of his four-year service, and his wife, Susan, moved with him wherever he went. "It wasn't dangerous. I liked it," he said. "I had a great job in the military and it had a lot to do with my success in business."

But although Carl's self-confidence benefited from his success in the armed forces, the transient lifestyle was a strain on his new marriage. Twice Susan left him and went back home to live with her parents. Neither separation lasted longer than a month. "She went home and stayed with her parents and realized that wasn't a real good idea either," Carl said.

In 1973, when Carl was 26, Susan gave birth to a daughter, Christina, while the couple was stationed in Hawaii. The responsibility of fatherhood, while at times overwhelming, was something Carl took very seriously. After he was discharged from the Army in 1974, the couple moved back to the Midwest, near the Chicago suburb where Susan had grown up. As a parent, Carl felt that quickly finding full-time work was a priority. "I thought about going back to school but that wasn't an option because I had a child," he said. Since he had held a part-time insurance sales job during college, he easily found a position selling insurance full-time, but hated it. He then took a job as a sales assistant in a large electronics store that sold stereos, televisions and other small home electronics items. Though Carl wasn't particularly looking for a retail job—"I just needed a job," he said—he soon realized he had found a good match for his skills. "When I started out I worked on the floor, then I became department manager and a lot of other stuff," he recalled.

Throughout the next decade, Carl stayed with the same electronics company, steadily rising through the ranks. "They put in a computer system in '79 and asked me if I wanted to be the number two guy in the department, coordinate inventory and stuff," he said, "About 6 months later I was about to kill the guy I worked for, so I applied for a buying position. After being told I wasn't qualified it was like, yeah, we'll give you a chance." As a buyer, Carl negotiated the purchase of nearly every piece of equipment sold in the company stores all over the country. Though he had applied to the job on a whim, Carl soon realized that large-scale purchasing was his perfect niche within the sales industry. "I love negotiating, making a deal," he said, "That's what I do, make deals."

Though Carl's career had begun to fall into place in his late twenties, his and Susan's marriage remained somewhat conflicted. The couple fought regularly, sometimes as often as twice a month ("pretty violent arguments," Carl admitted). Still, the fights were generally about smaller matters such as housekeeping. "I like strong-willed, powerful women, and Susan qualifies as that," said Carl, "There is a bad part with that good part." Carl was also unhappy with Susan's inability to keep the house clean and organized. "I think Susan is a wonderful mother and a terrible housekeeper," he commented, "She told me this morning that she had a cleaning crew coming in and I said, who can really clean this place? It is a disaster." Yet underlying the friction was a strong bond of mutual respect and common values. "Susan likes me because I'm honest. And I put up with some of her nuttiness," Carl joked, "I don't think either of us could imagine our lives without the other."

Carl's parents divorced when he was still in the Army. Throughout his twenties, his relationship to his parents continued to be extremely stressful. His feelings towards his father, whom he had respected when he was a teenager, were especially bitter. "My father's first granddaughter was born in Hawaii and he didn't come over. He didn't visit her for two and a half years," he said, "Then a year after I moved back to the States, he went to Hawaii with his girlfriend on a vacation. I never forgave him for that. Never."

When Carl was 31, his father, then just 58, was in a fatal auto accident. "The inquest ruled that the death was from injuries from an accident, but a normal person would have survived, "said Carl, "He had emphysema and after the accident, he never could breathe right again." Before he died, Carl's father spent three months in intensive care as his lungs slowly stopped functioning. Alternately furious and sad, Carl was unable to re-establish a connection with his father during that time. "I couldn't take it," he admitted. To Carl's relief, Susan stepped in and took over much of the day-to-day duty of visiting her father in law. "My father never got along with my wife, never liked her. I don't know why," Carl said, "She was always decent to him and liked him. But when he was dying, she would spend hours with him, hold his hand, communicate for two to three hours at a time." Carl greatly admired his wife's ability to be strong in a crisis. "Little things drive Susan crazy, make her an emotional basket case," he said, "When it is big, really serious, like someone dying, she can really come through."

Carl later admitted that the year his father died, 1979, was on the whole a "real rough time." Not only was he suffering from the loss of a parent, but his new position as a buyer—his first job with "real responsibility"—also caused him a significant amount of stress as he learned the ropes. With Susan's encouragement, he sought counseling from a pastor at a Lutheran church. Susan, who had been raised as a Lutheran, wanted to raise her children in the same religion, and Carl agreed that the children needed a religious background. But after his father's death, "Religion became something important to me as well," he said. Carl felt that the support of his wife and the church carried him through that difficult time. "If it wasn't for my wife, I wouldn't have a religion. I'd be nothing," he said, "My wife led me to religion, but never pushed. It is great." Later, Carl also credited religion with helping him be a better parent. "I think one of the reasons the kids are as great as they are is because they have had organized religion their whole lives," he said.

In 1981, Carl and Susan had another daughter, Jennifer. Around this time, Carl's mother's behavior became increasingly strange. "She had always done wacky stuff," he said, "She had over 300 pairs of shoes, and wore about eight. She had a thing about hiding money. She'd hide it in the waffle iron and burn it up when she turned the iron on. She burned up a bunch of savings bonds." It came as a surprise to Carl when his mother was diagnosed with senile dementia. "I just thought, whatever idiosyncrasies people have, the more pronounced they get as they get older," he said.

Carl's youngest child, a son, Peter, was born in 1985, when Carl was 37 years old. Peter was born with a birth defect—one of his legs was much shorter than the other—and was partially deaf. Later, he was also diagnosed with dyslexia. But Carl and Susan were determined to give their son the best opportunities possible, despite his disabilities. "He'll have a tough life, but we'll do everything to help him," said Carl, "There's a great line that my boss likes to say about our employees. He says, they ain't the best looking girls at the dance but I still love them."

From the moment his first child was born, Carl was determined to be a successful parent. "I wanted to be a better father than my father. My dad was an absent parent. I'm much more involved," he said. Carl also believed that having children tamed his wilder impulses. "I'd have no direction in my life without kids," he said. Since Susan worked outside the house only sporadically, most of the direct care of the children fell to her. But Carl stayed as involved as his work schedule allowed. "Susan arranges the birthday parties, but I'm always there," he said, "I do the camera and video stuff."

Throughout the 1980's, Carl's mother worsened, and eventually, he had no choice but to arrange for her to receive full-time nursing care. Since Carl had been an only child, his mother had given him power of attorney to handle all her assets. But shortly after he began making nursing home arrangements, Carl discovered that his mother had another child. "I didn't have any idea I had a half brother. He came up here to take her to Georgia to live with him. He said all he wanted was her money and he'd take her." Carl was skeptical about handing money over to a virtual stranger. "I told him it wasn't a good idea," he said. His intuition proved correct; within a year, his half-brother died of cancer. Unfortunately, negotiating the red tape of nursing home care and, later, state medical aid created a lot of stress for Carl. "You should see some of the correspondence I have with the Illinois Department of Public Aid," he said. After several years in the nursing home, his mother could no longer recognize him as her son. "She can't communicate at all, "said Carl, "Can't feed herself, go to the bathroom herself."

After eleven years in the nursing home, Carl's mother died. Having watched her painfully decline for so long, Carl felt only that the weight of responsibility for her care had been lifted. As an adopted child, he was not overly concerned that he might meet a similar fate. "Seeing my mother go through the mental thing, I'm kind of glad she wasn't my biological parent," he said, "That is good."

In 1990, at age 42, Carl had been working for the same company for over 15 years. But for the last two years, he found that he no longer enjoyed the work. "It was affecting my health—I was sick all the time," he said, "Fifteen years is long enough to work for one place." Carl decided to gamble on his future with the company. In a meeting with some of the company's top management, he asked for a promotion and threatened to quit if the request was not met. It wasn't. "They said, don't let the door hit you on the way out," he joked. Yet Carl had been careful not to gamble on his family's future. "I had a pension, profit sharing, 401(k)—I left with a lot of money," he said, "I figured if the worst case scenario came, I could get by."

After a few months of "playing golf and goofing off," Carl decided he wanted to work for a well-known stereo manufacturer. Instead, he was offered a sales position with a small, rival upstart stereo maker with a "real hot" product. "For a short period of time I made good money, then okay money," he said, "Then they began firing people." Carl soon found himself unemployed for the second time in eighteen months. "It was hard to find a job this time, there was a lot of downsizing going on," he said. But Carl's friendliness and resourcefulness led him to a new opportunity. A friend of his who was a real estate agent in the local area offered him a chance to try real estate sales. Carl had always avoided jobs that paid nothing except commission, but this time, decided to give it a try. "I was like, okay, I'll do it and keep looking for a real job," he said. To his surprise, he found he enjoyed the work. "I was five minutes from home, I had lived in the community for 13 years and knew a lot of people. The boss let everyone do whatever they wanted to do," he recalled.

After only eighteen months as a real estate agent, Carl got an unexpected call from an executive at another large electronics manufacturer who needed someone to head up the national procurement division. "In my mind I had said no more electronics, 17 years was enough," he said. The position would also require him and his family to relocate to Missouri. But the salary was compelling. "He asked, what would it take to bring you here and when I told him he kind of blanched," laughed Carl, "But then he said, when can you start."

When Carl was in his forties, he was astounded by what he had achieved in his life, both personally and professionally. "Today, to aspire to my position without a college degree is absolutely impossible. I don't interview people three levels below me without a college degree," he said, "I think I've overachieved, to tell the truth. I've had a little luck, a little being in the right place at the right time. I'm very honest." But though he often worked long hours, Carl never let his career ambitions prevent him from enjoying leisure activities like golf and bowling. "I am not work obsessed. Not at all. I am goofing off obsessed. That's what I do best," he said. Although he looked forward to retiring someday, he knew it would be some time before he could do so without sacrificing the lifestyle that he and his family had become accustomed to. "I have two nice cars, a membership at a tennis club and a wife that doesn't have to work," he said, "My family and I know if we sacrificed more in the next 15 years the reality of retiring at 60 would be there. I don't think it will be. It is worth it to have the things we want now."

Carl's children were a tremendous source of pride for him. "When it comes to child rearing, I say look at the results, we must have done something right," he said. Carl was particularly close with his eldest daughter, Christina, who, at 23, was living in New York, working as an intern in a law firm to prepare for law school. She had been a stellar student, graduating Phi Beta Kappa from a prestigious East Coast college. "Christina has done so much," Carl said proudly, "She is the kind of person that says, this is what I am going to do and does it. Really, she is wonderful." Even after Christina moved away from home, father and daughter remained close. "We talk on the phone at least twice a week," said Carl, "She even coaches me on how to deal with my wife. One of the best people I know."

Although Carl was not as close to his second daughter, Jennifer ("Jennifer is more emotional and introverted than her sister," he said, "I know nothing about her relationships, friends, virtually nothing."), he was consciously trying to develop the relationship. "I'm really trying to get closer to Jen and help her to plan what she wants to do with her life," Carl said, "She has no idea of where her life is going. But that's fine. She is a lovable, sweet kid."

Carl was also proud of the progress his son, Peter, had made despite his disabilities. "He is getting there, if the norm is 100, two years ago he was performing at 40. And now he is at 80," he said. Carl and Susan rarely, if ever, voiced disappointment with their son. "Peter will never achieve what the girls will from an academic standpoint, so we can never expect that from him," said Carl, "I always say we want you to be the best you can be. That is all anyone can ask. I think he likes that." Carl also genuinely enjoyed spending time with his son. "The majority of the time we spend together, we play," he said, "Read, talk, go for walks . . . I think we'll always be close. He's my boy."

As Carl and Susan entered their third decade of marriage, Carl found the relationship more relaxed and fulfilling than ever before. "We got pretty good at marriage," Carl joked. He felt he had become a better husband. "I think Susan likes it when I try to do things that she likes, just 'cause she likes them," he said. The frequency of the couple's arguments had decreased to just once a year. "Instead of arguing I go away and hide, go for a walk," Carl said, "We both want it that way, we don't want to hurt each other." Carl acknowledged that he was committed to the relationship for life. "My wife is still my best friend, it is really hokey," he said, "Even when we don't get along that well, I still think she is a real good friend. She is the person I want to be old with."

In his late forties, Carl bore little resemblance to his teenage self. As a teenager, he had been a perpetual underachiever, with low self-esteem due to the constant criticism of his parents. The adult Carl was capable and self-assured, with a solid, loving family life. He had overcome significant emotional hurdles to reach this point in his life, and yet Carl viewed none of his achievements as spectacular. To the contrary, he considered himself the epitome of a normal guy. "I'm not the worst person and I'm not the best," he said, "I like myself 80% of the time, and 10% of the time I despise myself. I think I'm an average grown up adolescent. When I'm 70, I'll be a normal geezer."

Carl appears to exemplify the essence of the normal teenager. An observer could have pointed to any number of causative factors had Carl become mentally ill: his having been adopted, the conflict between his parents as he was growing up, his mother's abusiveness, his father's emotional distance. But Carl, in fact, had the inner resources to transcend his background. He capitalized on his assets and learned to cope with his deficits. Perhaps that is the essence of normal adaptation.

At age 48, all three of the men we studied were doing well. Just as was true in their adolescence, none manifested marked psychiatric illness, criminality or emotional disturbance. They were successful in the most important areas in most person's lives: family, work, self-feelings, love for others, and role in the larger society. After 34 years, they seemed alike in their maturity, the differences in their adolescent adaptation apparently having been altered by the challenges and opportunities presented by progress into and through middle age.

Tony, Bob and Carl began their journey through adolescence into adulthood at quite different levels of adjustment. Yet each obtained, in middle age, a place in life redolent of good adjustment, self-confidence and strong family ties. As we will discuss, these men exemplify what our data show us in general: that within the normal range, adolescents, whatever their adaptive style in this stage, will, as they move through adulthood, reach toward a common high level of maturity and good adjustment.

NOTE

1. We are grateful to Cybelle Weisser, M.A., for writing this chapter.

Chapter 8

Longitudinal Studies
An Overview of the Literature[1]

Longitudinal studies are difficult and expensive to do. As a result, most often researchers of human development conduct cross-sectional studies, which are studies of contemporary groups or cohorts of persons differing from one another in age. In these studies, differences among the cohorts are taken to reflect how persons change as they get older.

One problem with cross-sectional studies is that cohorts can differ for all kinds of reasons other than just age. An obvious difference is generational. Teenagers today, for instance, were born and raised in a different era than were their middle-aged contemporaries including their parents. A cross-sectional study can leave us wondering whether differences between an adolescent cohort and a middle-aged cohort are due to their age difference or due to their generational difference. Cohorts can also differ by social class, education, ethnicity, and any number of other factors, all of which, simultaneously, are difficult to control.

Longitudinal studies avoid these difficulties. By looking at the same persons over time, alternative explanations of inter-group difference, such as generation or education level, are eliminated since persons are being compared only to them-selves. One difficulty in conducting longitudinal studies, however, is that they are expensive, and by definition take many years, often decades, to do. They also face the challenge of keeping in touch with and gaining the cooperation of the subjects over a long period of time (Vaillant, 2002).

Due to the difficulty inherent in conducting longitudinal studies, relatively few are extent. There are even fewer longitudinal studies that cover a time span of three decades or longer. In this chapter, we will review the findings of various long-term longitudinal studies most relevant to the development of normal males from adolescence into middle age.

In 1938, philanthropist William T. Grant provided funds to two student-health physicians at Harvard University to study healthy adult development (Bock and Heath, 1945: the "Harvard Study"). Heath (1945) selected 268 Harvard sophomore men for the research. Criteria for acceptance included a grade average of A or B, and having been described as psychologically healthy and "sound" by administrative staff and family interviews. Thereafter, each subject was interviewed by a psychiatrist about eight times. The interview focused on the subjects' family career plans and value systems.

In addition, an investigator studied each man's family in depth, traveling throughout the United States to meet their families. The thorough family history obtained included information about each man's relatives, social status, infant-child development, and family history of mental illness.

In 1967, George Vaillant joined the Harvard Study. Vaillant's focus has been the developmental influences that contribute to mental health and a subjective sense of well-being or, conversely, psychopathology through adulthood (Vaillant, 1974, 1977, 1983, 1998, 2000).

A major conclusion of Vaillant is that an individual's personality can significantly change over time. He further observed that adults sometimes remember events from their past quite differently from the way they reported them at the time the events took place. These findings, it should be noted, were based on subjective observations from interviews with the men.

It should be noted, in addition, that Vaillant only studied 37% of the original 268 Grant Study subjects. In 1977, Vaillant wrote that he selected 100 of the original 268 men; he then interviewed the 94 surviving men among the 100. From his description, it is not clear what criteria he used to select the 100 men in the first place. If one criterion was availability of information about these men, that would introduce a clear bias as to who was interviewed and who was not.

Two other well known longitudinal studies, are the Berkeley Guidance Study, which entailed following 252 infants born in an 18-month period beginning in 1929 (MacFarlane, 1938), and the Oakland Growth Study, which gathered data on 212 older subjects, fifth graders, also beginning in 1929 (Jones, 1938, 1939a, 1939b). When combined, the Berkeley Guidance/Oakland Growth Study comprised a total of 464 subjects (Block, 1971).

In 1971, Block located 170 of the 464 Berkeley Guidance/Oakland Growth subjects or 37% of them. Block's focus has been on enduring aspects of character. His methodology centered on the use of the Q-sort, a set of rules that guide a judge's evaluation of a subject's personality. Subjects' personalities were rated at different points in their lives. Judges were blind to one another's ratings allowing a test of inter-rater agreement.

In general, Block (1971, 1993) found that personality characteristics persist over time. To illustrate, among the men studied, the personality characteristic "self-defeating" correlated .46 from Junior High School to the mid-forties and "high aspiration level" correlated .45 over the same period of time. Among the women studied, "has fluctuating moods" correlated .40; "is cheerful" correlated .36; and "pushes limit" correlated .43. His findings further indicate that the atmosphere of a person's family strongly influences how that person turns out.

Block found too that several development types remained consistent from junior high through the mid-forties. Among male subjects, the major types were: "ego resilient," that is persons characterized by dependability, productivity, ambition, likeability, and wide interests; "unsettled under-controllers," that is persons characterized by impulsivity and changeableness, negativism, and under-control; and "vulnerable over-controllers," that is persons characterized by being over-controlled, constricted, uncomfortable with certainty, defeatist and introspective.

Clausen (1991, Clausen and Jones, 1998) used Block's cohorts from the Berkeley Guidance/Oakland Growth studies as well as 50 subjects from a third study, the Berkley Growth Study, a study that began with 62 infants born in 1929. Clausen studied personality changes related to assuming different roles over one's lifetime, personal commitments both marital and work-related, and losses of roles and commitments. Possible change-related variables were measured both in high school and in adulthood.

As reported by Clausen (1976, 1991, 1993), "planfully competent" persons manifest greater personality stability and, as adolescents, had a clear idea who they were. As teenagers, they understood the reality of their intellectual abilities, social skills and emotional responses to others. They used that understanding to interact with others in a responsible way. Planful competence, Clausen wrote, entailed the ability to make and keep commitments, and having sufficient self-confidence to pursue objectives in the face of obstacles.

Planful competence, in short, comprises good self-esteem, ego resilience and control, and realistic appraisal of one's intellectual ability. Competence in adolescence, Clausen found, is what led his subjects to be able to make realistic choices in life. This characteristic led to subjects' making wiser decisions with respect to their education, occupation, and marriage and, in general enabling them to lead more stable lives.

Qualifying Clausen's results is the fact that he studied relatively few of the subjects who had started with each of the three research samples he used. At 18 years of age, 41% of the original subjects had been lost to the study. Among those not lost, were some who were not considered lost if they had provided at least some data at age 18. If complete data collection was the criterion for being retained in the sample, then obviously an even higher percentage of the subjects would have been considered to have been lost.

In 1982, interviews were obtained from 61% of the subjects from the Berkeley Guidance and the Berkeley Growth Studies, who then were in their early 50's. That year the Adolescent Oakland Growth Study subjects were in their early 60's; only 42% of them were able to be interviewed.

In 1990, subjects from all three studies were again contacted through the use of a mail survey, when all the surviving subjects were in their early or late 60's. Data at this point were obtained from only 36% of the original subjects. It was not clear what percent of the subjects had passed away in the interim and hence were unavailable for study and what percent simply couldn't be found or had declined to participate.

Health (1991) recruited 80 17-year-old freshmen at Haverford College in Connecticut in the mid-1950's to participate in a longitudinal study. They were interviewed three times while in college, beginning in their Freshman year and continuing through their senior years. They were re-interviewed in the late 1960's when they were in their early 30's. In the 1980, Heath was able to re-contact 81% of the original 80 subjects.

Based on case studies, personality stability, Heath concluded, was more the norm than the exception. The character of the subjects' parents, Heath observed not their child-rearing techniques, influence how the children act and turn out. Unlike Vaillant, he found that his subjects' adult memories of their adolescence were reasonably accurate.

Caspi (2003) focused on the origins of, persistence of, and change in psychological traits over the life span using data from the Dunedin Multidisciplinary Health and Development Study in New Zealand. The study thus far has traced the development of a representative 1972 birth cohort of 1037 New Zealand men and women from the age of 3 to 26 (Caspi, 2002). According to Caspi and his collaborators, (Caspi, 1987; Caspi, 1998; Caspi, 2000), temperamental traits evident at birth have a life-long effect on development. Personality, Caspi found, shapes the social and environmental interactions an individual will seek or avoid. Caspi's ability to retain and follow-up with his subjects has been excellent. In 1998–1999, at the age of 26, 980 of the eligible 1,019 subjects, that is 96%, were still participating in the various studies.

In general, the various longitudinal studies we surveyed demonstrate significant continuity of personality throughout the life span. They differ on their emphasis on change within that framework. Block and Caspi emphasize stability of personality and personality characteristics; Vaillant, on the other hand, focuses on how persons change over time. Heath seems to occupy a middle position, finding continuity is more the norm than the exception. Clausen appears to believe that stability of personality itself is a characteristic of the person, specifically the "planfully competent" person. Presumably, persons who are not planfully competent are not as stable as those who are and might therefore show increasingly positive functioning with time, a possibility consistent with Vaillant's point of view.

A theme running through the review of these studies is that many suffer from marked attrition of the original subject pool. After the passage of many years, studies have lost as many as 60 to 65% of their subjects. Losing an appreciable number of subjects can lead to a number of problems. One problem, for example, is that only the most stable subjects may have stayed in the study. Generalizing from data provided by these subjects could lead to an overestimate of the stability of personality of the entire groups. This and other subjects connected to this review will be revisited in the Discussion section of this book.

NOTE

1. We are grateful to Emily Bennett, M.A., for contributing to this chapter.

Chapter 9

Normal Adolescent Boys as Adults
A Perspective

NORMAL MEN

As a group, normal men are below the radar of public scrutiny. They are not deviant or super heroes. They rarely are subject of movies or newspaper headlines. They are not fabulously wealthy. Their ambitions are circumscribed. They contribute to society, raise their children and respect other people. One could argue that they are the backbone and mainstream of American Society.

At age forty-eight, the vast majority of our subjects were doing well. They were all working. They had meaningful relationships with wives, children, and parents though less so with their siblings. They were contributing members of their communities. None of the 67 men studied manifested a major psychiatric illness.

That does not mean, however, that these men had sailed through life without experiencing significant adversity and painful emotional challenges. Each faced difficulties such as divorce, death of spouse or parents, illness, or loss of job.

Tony's life is illustrative of normal or "regular guy" development. He brought to adolescence many positive resources. He was favored by circumstances. He came from an intact loving family. As a child and teenager, he was encouraged and supported. He was gifted biologically in terms of physical appearance, intelligence, good health, and athleticism. His self-esteem as an adolescent was good. He was well adjusted; and he was moving smoothly through adolescence.

In adulthood, however, Tony reached the limit of his ability to cope. He turned to alcohol as a way to deal with his emotional pain. But Tony's alcoholism did not reflect a deep flaw in his personality or underlying psychopathology. Instead, it shows that no matter how well adjusted and how rich in resources, people have their emotional limits. For Tony, that limit was his highly stressful, heart rending work experiences.

Ironically, the very nature of the positive experiences that Tony had as a child and as a adolescent, may have left him less prepared than someone who had less favorable experiences would be to cope with life's adversities. This idea is consistent with the finding of Elder (1974) who found that economic hardship in adolescence had the positive effect of making people more resourceful in adulthood. Tony found himself overwhelmed and unable to cope, which was an unusual experience for him, and he turned to alcohol to help him get through it. Later, Tony had the emotional strength to look at himself, when he was at the nadir of his life, and realized he was on a short path to destruction. With the help of his wife, he was able to regain control of his life and stop drinking.

What is most salient about Tony's story is that, in the end, he had the resources to deal, not only with the emotional trauma that he experienced, but with the alcohol abuse that trauma engendered.

Our second life story, that of Bob illustrates the transition from being, in his case, a rather lost, undecided teenager to a mature, centered, self-confident adult. As we saw, when Bob was a youth, he was unpopular and lacked self-confidence. His grades were not that good. For a while he seemed to be going essentially nowhere. He seemed to do better in college and became what he described as a free thinker. He tried various drugs such as LSD. He wore his hair long; he espoused radical ideas. Yet when he graduated from college, he went to work for a brokerage house. In college he had a series of unsatisfying relationships with women. But in his senior year, he met a woman with whom he was able to develop a lasting meaningful and gratifying relationship.

Eventually, Bob's surgent adaptation led him to the cutting edge of technology. In other words, his willingness to explore paid off for him in the end. The teenager who seemed lost and had trouble establishing deep emotional connections became the man who loved his work and was centered in his relationship with his partner.

When we look at Carl, his story illustrates the ability of person's in the normal range to overcome a significant degree of adolescent emotional turmoil without the benefit of formal treatment. Carl brought many disadvantages to adolescence. He was adopted; he had an absentee father; his mother had been physically abusive to him; and his parents argued continuously and didn't like each other; all of which had an emotional impact on him as shown by his inclusion in the tumultuous group.

Yet Carl was able to be successful in the military. He married and had a stable marital relationship. He was a good father to his children. He was able to cope well with vocational set backs and he developed a good career. In other words,

Carl had the inner resources to transcend his background. In fact, Carl became as well functioning and normal as any of the other persons we studied.

It would be speculative to try to identify where Carl got these resources from, to say e.g., they were biological in origin or that his mother gave him emotional resources not reflected in her physical abusiveness. But whatever the origin of his resources, he had the ability to transcend and to reverse some of the experiences that he had. For example, having had an absentee father led Carl to resolve to be more involved with his own children, which became a source of great gratification for him. In that way, he was able to cope retrospectively with the negative experiences he had with his own father. He had the resilience to find through vocational success affirmation that may have been lacking in his childhood.

Carl, in particular, teaches us that, for people in the normal range, what appears to be adversity or negative aspects of functioning, can be transformed into their opposite. Part of the coping ability of the normal person is to take adversity or negative aspects of functioning and make something positive out of them.

Our data indicate that teenagers in the normal range adapt to and benefit from their life experiences. The emotions of the tumultuous teenager had become modulated. The surgent young man settled down. The continuous adolescent achieved a depth of adjustment through facing adversity that he never had before. As a result of their life experiences, our subjects reached a commonality of adaptation characterized by good adjustment in all salient aspects of their life.

OBESITY, MARIJUANA USE, SMOKING, AND DRINKING

Despite their overall good adjustment, our subjects were not consistently positive in all aspects of their functioning. Twenty-two percent are obese. Seven percent smoke marijuana at least once a week. Eighteen percent smoke at least a pack of cigarettes a day. Fifteen percent consume a relatively large amount of alcohol, three or more drinks a day. Five percent consume six or more drinks a day.

Do these facts reflect some sign of deeper emotional disturbance in our subjects? Our thought instead is that these facts are more reflective of the state of our society and culture than they are of individual psychological dysfunction. The prevalence of obesity, alcohol use, and smoking among our subjects is consistent with national data pertaining to contemporary middle-aged men.

National statistics report that 23.2% of men 45 to 54 years of age were obese between 1988 and 1994 (CDC, National Center for Health Statistics).

About 5% of persons 12 or older, 2001 national statistics indicate, used marijuana during the month immediately prior to the survey interview (Office of Applied Studies, 2001 National Household Survey on Drug Abuse, U.S. Department of Health and Human Services).

The median prevalence of smoking among adults in 2001 was 23.4% as shown by data from the National Center for Chronic Disease Prevention and Health Promotion. (The data indicate that smoking prevalence among men and women is comparable.)

National statistics (National Institute on Alcohol Abuse and Alcoholism) showed 5% of non-black males ages 45–54 suffered from alcohol abuse or dependence in 1992.

These data reflect the differences between normality as average as normality as health (Offer and Sabshin, 1984). Obesity, using marijuana, smoking cigarettes, and drinking more than a moderate amount of alcohol is not statistically unusual in contemporary American society. Yet medical data show that obesity, cigarette smoking, and alcohol abuse in particular present significant health risks. Persons can engage in behavior that is statistically and culturally normal, yet is highly liable to harm them medically.

TRADITIONAL GENDER ROLE

The vast majority of our subjects were either married or living with a romantic partner when interviewed as adults. Most of these persons were highly satisfied with their relationships. Their responses made clear that, despite the "sexual revolution" that occurred in America beginning in the 1960's, the relationship of the married men with their wives resounded in tradition. According to these men, their wives, much more than they, performed a traditional domestic role involving doing the cooking, washing the dishes, doing the laundry, cleaning the house, and doing the grocery shopping.

Apparently the primary role of the men, again in conformance with tradition, is to maintain the outside upkeep of the house such as tending the lawn and earn income. It should be pointed out that many of these men's wives worked outside the home. There have been many reports indicating that women who work full-time continue to perform a disproportionate share of household duties. Our data and these studies make clear that traditional cultural attitudes and roles are not easily changed despite the efforts and the eloquence of the partisans of the women's movement. Normality and tradition are intertwined and societal evolution must come slowly.

ADULT MEMORY

A key finding in this book concerns the accuracy of adult person's memories of their adolescence. One aspect of normality, we found, was that well-adjusted adults do not remember their adolescence very well. Our data show that there is essentially no correlation between what our subjects as adults thought and felt about their adolescence and what they actually thought and felt as adolescents. Further analysis revealed that many of our subjects tended to misremember their adolescence by making it more of a reflection of the cultural stereotype of the teenage years and either more or less idyllic in many cases then it actually was.

To illustrate stereotyping, 44% of the adult subjects believed that when they were teenagers they felt sexual intercourse was okay anytime during high school. In fact only 15% of the subjects felt this way when they were teenagers. Our subjects seem to have assimilated their adolescent experience to a stereotype of the promiscuous adolescent that in fact did not pertain.

Another example of stereotyping in their adolescence is their recall of whether religion was helpful to them. Seventy-four percent of our subjects as adults said no, it was not helpful. In fact, when they were adolescents, 70% of our subjects said yes to this question. In this case, our subjects appear to have assimilated their adolescence to a stereotype of teenagers as not being interested in or involved with religion.

The response to the item, "Who was your mother's favorite?" illustrates the tendency of our subjects to idealize their adolescence. As teenagers, 14% identified themselves as their mother's favorite. As adults, 30% of our subjects identify themselves as having been the favorite of their mother. (Interestingly no such trend occurred in respect to their father.)

These data also may reflect what Schacter (2001) called the "sin of bias." The "sin of bias" entails a person's filtering recollections of past events using current knowledge. As Schacter stated (p. 138), "our memories of the past are often re-scripted to fit with our present views and needs."

This sin of bias can further help us understand why our subjects were more likely as adults to see themselves when they were adolescents as their mother's favorite than they actually were. It is of interest to note that our subjects, as adults, by in large reported excellent relationships with their mothers. Their narrative as adults may reflect their current relationship with their mother more than their actual teenage relationship with her.

Our subjects, however, appear to have de-idealized their adolescence with respect to discipline. As a case in point, 51% of the subjects when teenagers identified the discipline they received as not consistent. In contrast, 83% of the subjects when adults believed the discipline they received was not consistent. Clearly, the subjects as adults remembered their feelings about the discipline they received as being considerably more negative than actually was the case.

There also was a marked change with respect to their beliefs about what the worst thing about their home life was. In their teenage years, 40% of the subjects identified physical comfort as the worst thing about their home life; but as adults, 83% recalled emotional comfort or overt family conflict as the worst thing about their home life.

These data are consistent with other points made by Daniel Schacter (2001), as well as points made by Dan McAdams (1993), and Bert Cohler (1981). As Schacter pointed out, "the sin of transience" reflects the tendency of persons to forget experiences with the passage of time. He points out that a common result of transience is that after months or years there is an extent of forgetting "that leaves in its wake scattered shards of experience:" (p. 33). This sin appears to have characterized our subjects' inability to accurately recall their perceptions and attitudes as adolescents.

Our subjects' self-narrative included their being the recipient, when they were teenagers, of more negative discipline than actually was the case. Schacter makes the point that one way memory gets distorted is through the phenomena of "the sin of persistence." Persistence refers to a person's tendency to remember emotional salient events more clearly and at greater length than events that are less emotionally compelling. It is possible that our subjects recall the discipline they received more vividly than most events in their adolescence. As a result, those memories form a disproportionate subset of the total memories they have of their teenage years leading them to believe that the discipline they received was more strict and more unfair than it actually was.

Consistent with Schacter's views, McAdams (1993) stated that, "the personal myth continues to develop and change through most of our adult years" (p. 14). McAdams defines a personal myth as a special kind of story that each of us constructs to make our lives into a purposeful and convincing whole.

Cohler (1981) described the importance of the creation of a personal narrative for each person about his or her life. According to Cohler, the person develops a narrative, "which provides the most coherent or internally consistent account of the life course" (p. 406). He suggests that there is more concern with the adequacy of the narrative than with the actuality of the events of the person's life. Earlier memories change, Cohler asserts, "together with the changing context of time and situation, these earlier memories are continually revised so as to maintain a sense of continuity across the life course."

The perspectives of Cohler, McAdams, and Schacter help us understand the role of stereotyping in leading to our subjects' memory distortions. To make sense of their lives, our subjects tended to look back on themselves as adolescents as being like typical teenagers, but typical teenagers as they were viewed in the late 1990's, not as they actually functioned in the early 1960's. Our subjects' views of their adolescence appear to have been filtered through their stereotype of what adolescents were like 34 years ago or are like now.

STABILITY OF PERSONALITY

The emphasis of Block is on stability of personality through time. His focus is on traits that persist through the lifetime of the individual. Our work emphasizes a different aspect of human functioning. One can have the same personality trait, but it can serve different functions in different decades of life. If Block were to look at Bob, he might see a person who remains a risk taker and an innovator. Our focus is on Bob having used that trait in a very different way as a mature adult than he did as a teenager. When he was a teenager, taking risks meant espousing rebellious ideas, experimenting with drugs, and experimenting with different relationships with women. As a mature adult, risk taking meant venturing into self-employment, seeking the cutting edge of technology, and establishing a 25-year non-marital yet ever deepening relationship with a woman.

Vaillant has taken the position that "Defenses evolve into more mature styles." We believe this position is consistent with our view that the normal individual, no matter what his style or level of coping was as a youth, moves toward increasing maturity, inner stability, and more satisfactory interpersonal relationships. There is a modulation of the traits of youth toward centeredness, a feeling of ease or accommodation with one's self, significant others, employment, and the larger society.

"ADOLESCENT TURMOIL"

As noted earlier in this book, our work stands in contrast to the "sturm and drung" theories of early psychoanalytic thinkers. Those theories reflected the ideology that persons struggle to control unacceptable impulses and that there is a thin line between the normal and the abnormal person. "Normality" in this view is a fragile cover overlaying a caldron of raging, socially unacceptable impulses. To some psychoanalytic thinkers, there is always the possibility that normal adjustment conceals pathology. The person may look well adjusted but either may not be in touch with, or be repressing his underlying maladjustment. Persons might seem to be functioning well, but in actuality are not because they may not have resolved various childhood conflicts.

In 1962, when the senior author (Offer, 1969; Offer and Offer 1975) began to study normal teenagers, the phrase "normal teenager" was considered an oxymoron. People either thought there was no such phenomenon or believed that the idea represented a misperception or misunderstanding of adolescents. To accept the idea of normality among adolescents required a paradigm shift in thinking, not only about that stage of life, but about normal adjustment in general.

In this book, we have demonstrated that the normal adolescents identified by Offer in the 1960's and 1970's continue to manifest normal functioning into their late forties.

Their barely repressed raging impulses never broke through because, the data shows, that they never represented these men's inner experience. The metaphor of the raging id, barely controlled by a fragile ego and rigid and vulnerable superego (or conscience) does not apply to the lives of the men we studied. The evidence for their having experienced deep emotional turmoil or "sturm and drung" simply isn't there. In other words, our data does not reflect the model of an ego and a super ego struggling to master and bring into conformance an unruly and powerful id. In adolescence, when theoretically the id is revitalized by the surges of impulses and drives that come with puberty, our subjects were not in marked emotional turmoil but rather leading a life that was a precursor to the normal and stable life they were to have as adults.

Our data suggests that normal persons do not struggle with raging impulses, but instead reach a balance early in life between personal desires and drives and the demands and expectations of their family and the larger society. This balance is achieved naturally and without turmoil, is robust and stable, and probably characterizes the vast majority of persons.

This may come as a surprise to many clinicians whose life experience, and in particular their professional experience, has been dominated by conflictual relationships and adaptations. For many mental health professionals, there is a professional bias to the effect that only persons who have been through psychotherapy or psychoanalysis can be well adjusted. For these professionals, persons, who appear to be well adjusted and who have not been through psychotherapy or psychoanalysis, are fragile because they are always in danger of experiencing, in an adverse way, their unresolved conflicts. A man like Carl could only exist in fiction. But in fact, he had never been in treatment, yet he was able to transcend the many difficulties he faced as a child.

THE THREE ROUTES THROUGH ADOLESCENCE

Offer and Offer's (1975) earlier work showed that there were three normal routes through adolescence. In this study, we found that the distinctions reflected by the three routes largely were obviated by the passage of time. The only significant difference among our subjects reflective of the three routes was with respect to family relationships. The Continuous subjects had had the most positive family experiences as children and, as adults, tended to replicate the positive experiences in this area that they had had.

As noted, by age 48, all of our subjects were doing well in all facets of their life no matter what path they had taken through adolescence and young adulthood. Our data indicates that teenagers in the normal range adapt to and benefit from their life experiences. The emotions of the tumultuous teenager became modulated. The surgent young man settled down. The continuous adolescent achieved a depth of adjustment through facing adversity that he never had before. As a result of their life experiences, our subjects reached a commonality of adaptation characterized by good adjustment in all salient aspects of their life.

A METHODOLOGICAL NOTE

This study illustrates the advantages of studying one group of persons in-depth over the course of decades. Studying persons repeatedly through intensive interviews, qualitatively as well as quantitatively, moves research away from abstract, isolated data to the warp and weave of subjects' individual lives. People adjust, struggle, triumph, suffer, and experience joy. They cannot be captured with any semblance of their subjective actuality through the use of simple categories or measurements taken at only one point or one stage of their life.

Important too is to comment on the great advantages of obtaining cooperation across time from all or almost all of the subjects originally studied. In this work, we had the good fortune to obtain the cooperation, 34 years after the study began, of 94% of the living original subjects. As we commented earlier, dropouts are the bane of many longitudinal studies. A large dropout rate inevitably casts doubt on the validity of longitudinal findings since, it always has to be conceded, those who dropped out might be very different from those who remained. It might even be true that those who dropped out are diametrically opposite to those who remained, thus negating any findings that were made. A 94% retention rate across decades is unusual for this type of study and assures that our findings do characterize this group accurately. This retention rate also reflects the character of our subjects, which as a group resounds in commitment, stability, and social responsibility. These men know how to give, and that, our findings suggest, is part of being normal.

Appendix A

Representations of the Data: Figures 1–69

Yes 33%   No 67%

Figure 1. Percent who served in the military.

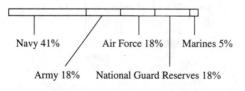

Navy 41%   Air Force 18%   Marines 5%

Army 18%   National Guard Reserves 18%

Figure 2. Branch of service served.

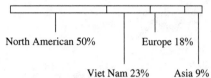

North American 50%   Europe 18%

Viet Nam 23%   Asia 9%

Figure 3. Where served.

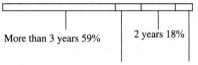

More than 3 years 59%   2 years 18%

3 years 14%   1 years 9%

Figure 4. Length of service.

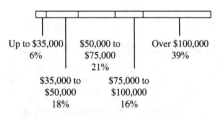

Up to $35,000 $50,000 to   Over $100,000
6% $75,000   39%
                       21%

$35,000 to $75,000 to
$50,000 $100,000
18%   16%

Figure 5. Income.

Professional/Technical	50%
Managers/Officials	24%
Proprietors	4%
Clerical	2%
Sales	4%
Craftsmen/foremen	2%
Un/semiskilled	13%
Service	2%

Socioeconomic profile of the wives of the married men

Professional/Technical	41%
Managers/Officials	11%
Clerical	7%
Sales	4%
Craftsmen/foremen	4%
Un/semiskilled	2%
Not working outside home	30%

Figure 6. Socioeconomic profile of married men.

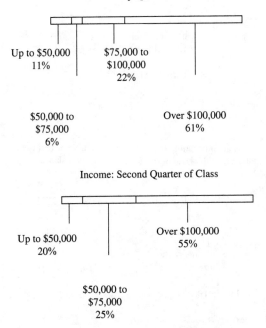

Income: Top Quarter of Class

Up to $50,000
11%

$75,000 to
$100,000
22%

$50,000 to
$75,000
6%

Over $100,000
61%

Income: Second Quarter of Class

Up to $50,000
20%

Over $100,000
55%

$50,000 to
$75,000
25%

Figure 7. Association between class standing in senior year high school and income level at age 48
$r = -.285^*$, (N = 63) Pearson correlation $p < 0.01$; negative correlation shows an association between higher income and better class standing.

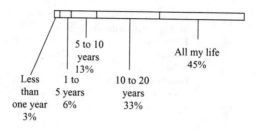

Figure 8. How long doing this type of work.

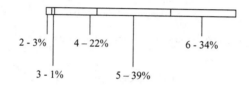

*1 - Dislike work very much   6 - Like work very much

*(On a scale from 1 to 6, scale point1
was not endorsed by any subject)

Figure 9. Like/dislike work.

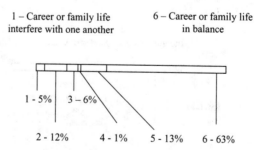

Figure 10. Balance between family life and career.

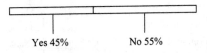

Yes 45%   No 55%

Figure 11. Any unemployment during adulthood for more than a month.

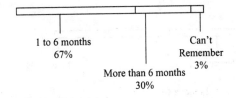

1 to 6 months   Can't
67%   Remember
                                 3%
              More than 6 months
              30%

Figure 12. Unemployed for how long.

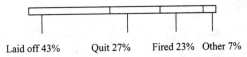

Laid off 43%   Quit 27%   Fired 23%   Other 7%

Figure 13. Cause of unemployment when unemployed.

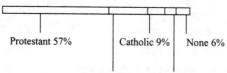

Figure 14. Religion of subjects.

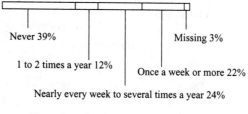

Figure 15. Church or synagogue attendance.

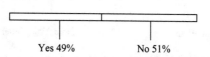

Figure 16. Have enough leisure time.

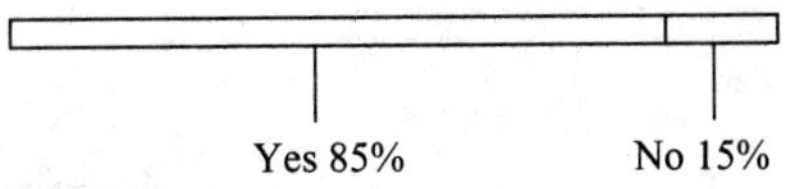

Yes 85%   No 15%

Figure 17. Takes vacations.

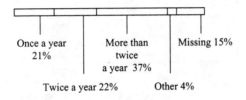

Once a year   More than   Missing 15%
21%   twice
                                a year 37%

Twice a year 22%   Other 4%

Figure 18. Frequency of vacations.

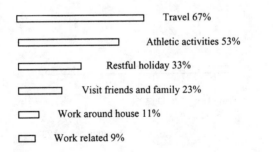

Travel 67%

Athletic activities 53%

Restful holiday 33%

Visit friends and family 23%

Work around house 11%

Work related 9%

Figure 19. How vacations are spent (Subject could give multiple answers.)

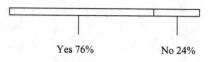

Yes 76%   No 24%

Figure 20. Mother alive.

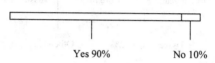

Yes 90%   No 10%

Figure 21. Percent of mothers healthy and living independently.

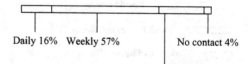

Daily 16%   Weekly 57%   No contact 4%

Monthly or Less 23%

Figure 22. How often in contact with mother.

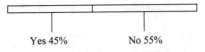

Yes 45%   No 55%

Figure 23. Father alive.

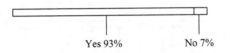

Yes 93%   No 7%

Figure 24. Percent of fathers healthy and living independently.

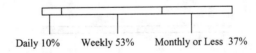

Daily 10%   Weekly 53%   Monthly or Less 37%

Figure 25. How often in contact with father.

1 – Did not get along   6 – Got along very well

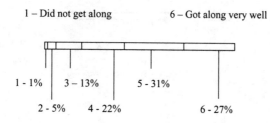

1 - 1%   3 – 13%   5 - 31%

2 - 5%   4 - 22%   6 - 27%

Figure 26. Rating, as an adult, of relationship with mother when in high school.

*1 – Did not get along   6 – Got along very well

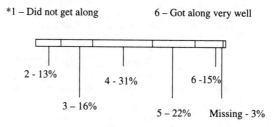

2 - 13%

4 - 31%   6 -15%

3 – 16%

5 – 22%   Missing - 3%

*(On a scale of 1 to 6, scale point 1 was not
endorsed by any subject)

Figure 27. Rating, as an adult, of relationship with father when in high school.

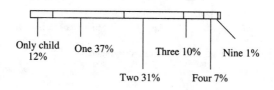

Only child   One 37%   Three 10%   Nine 1%
12%

Two 31%   Four 7%

Total # of siblings: 117

Figure 28. How many siblings do you have.

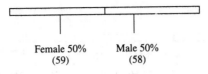

Female 50%   Male 50%
(59)   (58)

Figure 29. Sex of siblings.

1 - Not close at all   6 - Very close

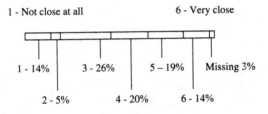

1 - 14%   3 - 26%   5 – 19%   Missing 3%

2 - 5%   4 - 20%   6 - 14%

Figure 30. How close to all siblings.

1 - Not close at all   6 - Very close

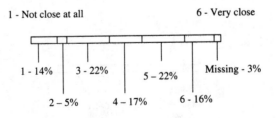

1 - 14%   3 - 22%   5 – 22%   Missing - 3%

2 – 5%   4 – 17%   6 - 16%

Figure 31. How close to males sibling.

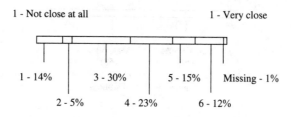

1 - Not close at all   1 - Very close

1 - 14%   3 - 30%   5 - 15%   Missing - 1%

2 - 5%   4 - 23%   6 - 12%

Figure 32. How close to female sibling.

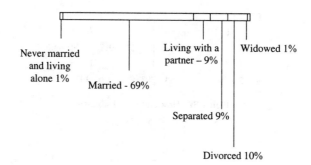

Never married
and living
alone 1%   Living with a   Widowed 1%
                    partner – 9%
          Married - 69%

                    Separated 9%

                Divorced 10%

Figure 33. Current marital status.

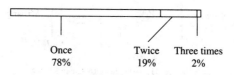

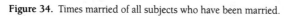

Once   Twice   Three times
78%   19%   2%

Figure 34. Times married of all subjects who have been married.

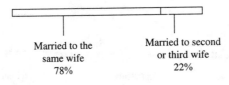

Figure 35. Of those who are currently married (46), how many are married to the same woman.

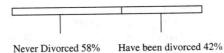

Figure 36. Of those who have been married, how many have ever been divorced.

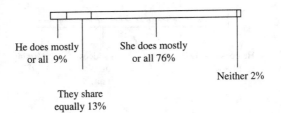

Figure 37. Who does the cooking.

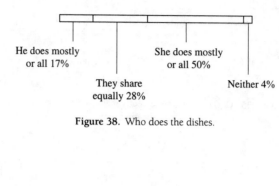

He does mostly
or all 17%

She does mostly
or all 50%

They share
equally 28%

Neither 4%

Figure 38. Who does the dishes.

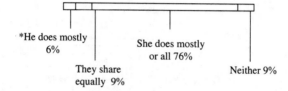

*He does mostly
6%

She does mostly
or all 76%

They share
equally 9%

Neither 9%

*(He does all was not endorsed by any subject.)

Figure 39. Who does the laundry.

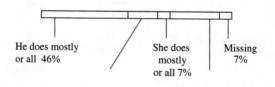

He does mostly
or all 46%

She does
mostly
or all 7%

Missing
7%

They share
equally 15%

Service or
other 26%

Figure 40. Who cares for the lawn.

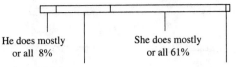

He does mostly
or all 8%

She does mostly
or all 61%

They share
equally 28%

Neither 2%

Figure 41. Who does the grocery shopping.

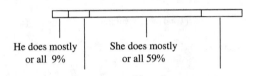

He does mostly
or all 9%

She does mostly
or all 59%

They share
equally 11%

Service or
housekeeper 22%

Figure 42. Who does the house cleaning.

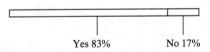

Yes 83%

No 17%

Figure 43. Personal choice to be childless (among those without children.)

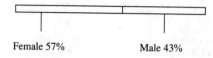

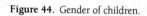

Female 57%   Male 43%

Figure 44. Gender of children.

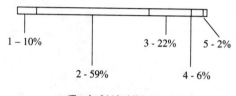

1 – 10%   3 - 22%   5 - 2%

2 - 59%   4 - 6%

(Total of 113 children)

Figure 45. If children, number of children each has.

1 – Very Poor   6 – Excellent

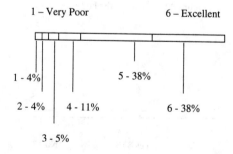

1 - 4%   5 - 38%

2 - 4%   4 - 11%   6 - 38%

3 - 5%

Figure 46. Relationship rating with children (Rating of each of 113 children.)

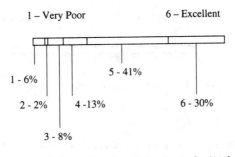

Figure 47. Rating of relationship with children by gender (64 daughters.)

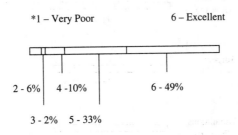

*(On a scale from 1 to 6, scale point 1 was not
endorsed by any subject.)

Figure 48. Rating of relationship with children by gender (49 sons.)

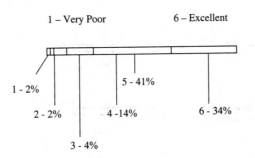

Figure 49. Rating of relationship with pre school through high school age
children (58 children.)

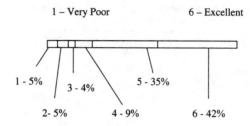

1 – Very Poor   6 – Excellent

1 - 5%   3 - 4%   5 - 35%

2- 5%   4 - 9%   6 - 42%

Figure 50. Rating of relationship with adult children (older than 18 years of age)
(55 children.)

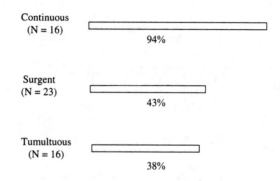

Continuous
(N = 16)

94%

Surgent
(N = 23)

43%

Tumultuous
(N = 16)

38%

Figure 51. Percent married and never divorced.

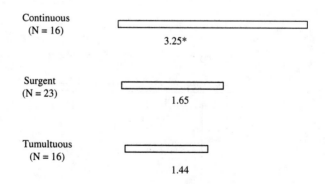

Continuous
(N = 16)

3.25*

Surgent
(N = 23)

1.65

Tumultuous
(N = 16)

1.44

F (anova) (2/52 d.f) = 9.43
P<.0003
*the higher the score, the more traditional the family

Figure 52. Analysis of traditional family scores of three routes groups.

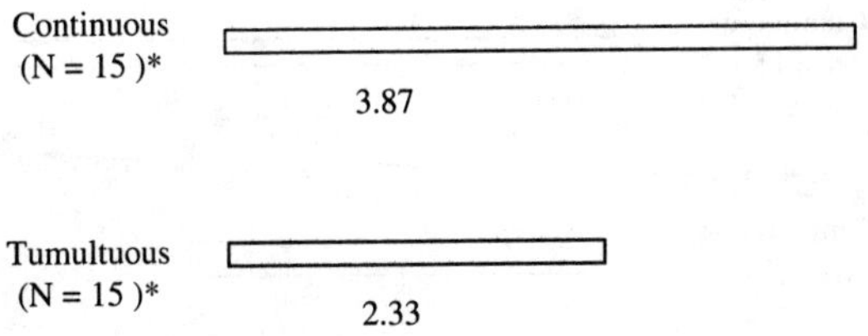

Continuous
(N = 15)*
3.87

Tumultuous
(N = 15)*
2.33

t Test (28d.f.) = 1.87
P<.05, 1 tailed.

*One person did not answer. The higher the score, the more
frequently the person attended religious services.

Figure 53. Comparison of continuous and tumultuous groups with respect to
attendance at religious services.

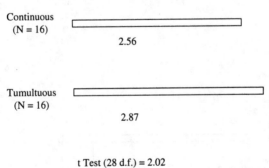

Continuous
(N = 16)
2.56

Tumultuous
(N = 16)
2.87

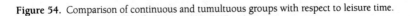

t Test (28 d.f.) = 2.02
P<.05, 1 tailed

Figure 54. Comparison of continuous and tumultuous groups with respect to leisure time.

Continuous
(N = 15)*

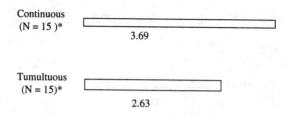

3.69

Tumultuous
(N = 15)*

2.63

t Test (28d.f.) = 2.08
P<.05
*One person did not answer.

Figure 55. Comparison of continuous and tumultuous groups with respect
to frequency of exercise.

Yes 70%   No 30%

Figure 56. Do they exercise.

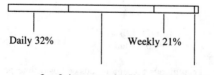

Daily 32%   Weekly 21%

2 to 3 times a week 45%   Occasionally 2%

Figure 57. If yes, how often do they exercise.

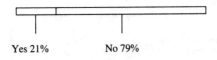

Yes 21%   No 79%

Figure 58. Do they smoke cigarettes.

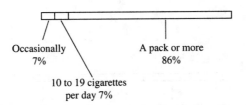

Occasionally   A pack or more
7%   86%

10 to 19 cigarettes
per day 7%

Figure 59. If yes, how much do they smoke.

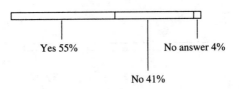

Yes 55%   No answer 4%

No 41%

Figure 60. If does not currently smoke, did they ever smoke.

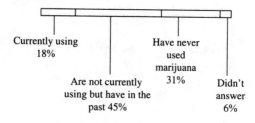

Currently using
18%

Are not currently
using but have in the
past 45%

Have never
used
marijuana
31%

Didn't
answer
6%

Figure 61. Overview of marijuana use.

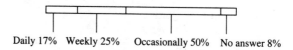

Daily 17%   Weekly 25%   Occasionally 50%   No answer 8%

Figure 62. Of those smoking marijuana (12 subjects or 18% of the sample),
how often did they smoke.

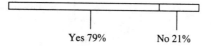

Yes 79%   No 21%

Figure 63. Do subjects have an active sex life.

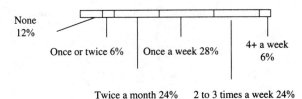

None
12%

Once or twice 6% | Once a week 28% | 4+ a week 6%

Twice a month 24%   2 to 3 times a week 24%

Figure 64. How often have subjects had sex in the last 12 months.

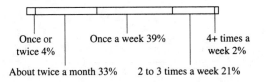

Once or twice 4%   Once a week 39%   4+ times a week 2%

About twice a month 33%   2 to 3 times a week 21%

Figure 65. Frequency of sex of married men in the past 12 months.

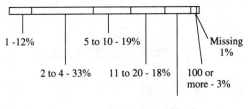

1 -12%   5 to 10 - 19%   Missing 1%

2 to 4 - 33%   11 to 20 - 18%   100 or more - 3%

21 to 99 - 13%

Figure 66. Number of partners of all subjects in lifetime.

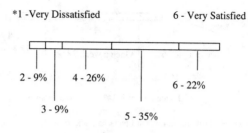

*(On a scale from 1 to 6, scale point 1 was not
endorsed by any subject.)

Figure 67. Married men's satisfaction with current sex life.

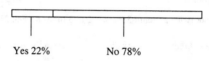

Figure 68. Romantic relationship outside of marriage of married men (based on the 64 subjects
who are currently or had been married.)

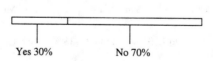

Figure 69. Has been unfaithful to wife during marriage (based on the 64 subjects
who are currently or had been married.)

Subjects' Offer Self-Image Questionnaire Endorsements At Age 14 (N = 67)

Scale # 1. Emotional tone

	Describes me very well	Describes me well	Describes me fairly well	Does not describe me	Does not really describe me	Does not describe me at all
1. I feel tense most of the time.	3%	0%	5%	20%	47%	26%
2. I feel inferior to most people I know.	0%	0%	5%	15%	35%	45%
3. Most of the time I am happy.	27%	42%	24%	5%	0%	2%
4. My feelings are easily hurt.	0%	3%	20%	25%	38%	14%
5. I feel relaxed under normal circumstances.	40%	35%	12%	8%	2%	3%
6. I am so very anxious.	8%	17%	26%	23%	17%	9%
7. I feel so very lonely.	2%	0%	2%	3%	47%	47%
8. I enjoy life.	47%	50%	2%	0%	0%	2%
9. Even when I am sad I can enjoy a good joke.	22%	29%	39%	6%	3%	2%
10. I frequently feel sad.	0%	3%	6%	9%	50%	32%

Scale # 2. Impulse control

	Describes me very well	Describes me well	Describes fairly me well	Does not describe me	Does not really describe me	Does not describe me at all
1. I carry many grudges.	0%	2%	8%	21%	52%	18%
2. I "lose my head" easily.	6%	5%	12%	26%	24%	27%
3. At times I have fits of crying and/or laughing that I seem unable to control.	2%	3%	3%	5%	17%	71%
4. I can take criticism without resentment.	12%	15%	33%	18%	14%	8%
5. I get violent if I don't get my way.	2%	0%	6%	14%	47%	32%
6. Even under pressure I manage to remain calm.	3%	28%	46%	14%	5%	5%
7. I keep an even temper most of the time.	13%	30%	42%	11%	5%	0%
8. I fear something constantly.	2%	3%	9%	9%	35%	42%
9. Usually I control myself.	18%	59%	17%	3%	3%	0%

Scale # 3. Mental Helath

	Describes me very well	Describes me well	Describes fairly me well	Does not describe me	Does not really describe me	Does not describe me at all
1. When I am with people, I am afraid someone will make fun of me.	0%	0%	14%	19%	31%	37%
2. I am confused most of the time.	2%	2%	6%	5%	50%	36%
3. I often blame myself even when I am not at fault.	0%	11%	11%	29%	32%	18%
4. Sometimes I feel so ashamed of myself that I just want to hide in a corner and cry.	5%	2%	9%	12%	38%	35%
5. I feel empty emotionally most of the time.	0%	3%	9%	17%	41%	30%
6. I often feel that I would rather die than go on living.	2%	0%	6%	9%	19%	64%
7. Other people are not after me to take advantage of me.	9%	35%	26%	11%	14%	5%
8. Even though I am continuously on the go, I seem unable to get things done.	3%	6%	14%	14%	48%	14%
9. I believe I can tell the real from the fantastic.	27%	38%	27%	5%	2%	2%
10. When I enter a new room I have a strange and funny feeling.	5%	8%	16%	22%	28%	22%
11. When I am with people, I am bothered by hearing strange noises.	0%	0%	3%	8%	28%	62%
12. I do not have many fears which I cannot understand.	12%	41%	36%	5%	6%	0%
13. No one can harm me just by not liking me.	15%	35%	23%	15%	9%	3%

Scale # 4. Social Functioning

	Describes me very well	Describes me well	Describes me fairly well	Does not describe me	Does not really describe me	Does not describe me at all
1. I usually feel out of place at picnics and parties.	2%	2%	9%	15%	49%	24%
2. I think that other people just don't like me.	0%	2%	8%	12%	47%	32%
3. I find it extremely hard to make friends.	2%	0%	2%	9%	47%	41%
4. I do not mind being corrected, since I can learn from it.	19%	43%	24%	10%	2%	3%
5. I prefer being alone than with other kids my age.	3%	8%	8%	3%	26%	52%
6. If others disapprove of me I get terribly upset.	2%	5%	11%	20%	50%	13%
7. Being together with older people gives me a good feeling.	33%	58%	6%	2%	2%	0%
8. I do not have a particularly difficulty time in making friends.	26%	36%	26%	3%	9%	0%
9. I enjoy most parties I go to.	32%	52%	17%	0%	0%	0%

Scale # 5. Family Functioning

	Describes me very well	Describes me well	Describes me fairly well	Does not describe me	Does not really describe me	Does not describe me at all
1. I think that I will be a source of pride to my parents in the future.	15%	47%	33%	2%	2%	2%
2. My parents are almost always on the side of someone else, such as my brother or sister.	6%	8%	9%	17%	27%	33%
3. My parents will be disappointed in me in the future.	0%	0%	0%	2%	39%	60%
4. Very often I feel that my father is no good	0%	0%	2%	5%	11%	83%

(Continued)

Scale # 5. (*Continued*)

	Describes me very well	Describes me well	Describes me fairly well	Does not describe me	Does not really describe me	Does not describe me at all
5. Understanding my parents is beyond me.	2%	2%	14%	21%	44%	18%
6. I can count on my parents most of the time.	29%	37%	9%	8%	6%	11%
7. Most of the time my parents get along well with each other.	55%	23%	8%	5%	2%	9%
8. When my parents are strict I feel that they are right even if I get angry.	20%	27%	27%	9%	14%	3%
9. When I grow up and have a family it will be in at least a few ways similar to my own.	14%	39%	35%	8%	0%	5%
10. I feel that I have a part in making family decisions.	15%	31%	37%	7%	10%	2%
11. My parents are usually patient with me.	20%	47%	27%	3%	3%	0%
12. Very often parents don't understand because they had an unhappy childhood.	3%	0%	9%	25%	34%	28%
13. Usually I feel that I am a bother at home.	3%	5%	9%	9%	48%	26%
14. I like one of my parents much better than the other.	5%	0%	9%	3%	17%	66%
15. My parents are ashamed of me.	0%	2%	2%	3%	24%	70%
16. I try to stay away from home most of the time.	0%	3%	9%	9%	48%	31%
17. I have been carrying a grudge against my parents for years.	0%	0%	0%	3%	19%	79%
18. Most of the time my parents are satisfied with me.	18%	46%	32%	0%	5%	0%
19. Very often I feel that my mother is no good.	0%	0%	5%	3%	17%	76%

Scale # 6. Vocational Attitudes

	Describes me very well	Describes me well	Describes me fairly well	Does not describe me	Does not really describe me	Does not describe me at all
1. I feel that working is too much responsibility for me.	0%	3%	0%	9%	33%	55%
2. Only stupid people work.	0%	2%	0%	0%	5%	94%
3. I am sure that I will be proud about my future profession.	40%	43%	14%	2%	2%	0%
4. I would rather sit around and loaf off than work.	5%	6%	12%	22%	28%	28%
5. At times I think about what kind of work I will do in the future.	47%	36%	14%	3%	0%	0%
6. I would rather be supported for the rest of my life than work.	3%	3%	5%	17%	22%	50%
7. A job well done gives me pleasure.	58%	36%	6%	0%	0%	0%
8. I feel that there is plenty that I can learn from others.	34%	46%	14%	3%	2%	2%
9. At times, I feel like a leader and feel that other kids can learn something from me.	11%	23%	35%	22%	6%	3%
10. School and studying mean very little to me.	2%	2%	2%	11%	20%	65%

Scale # 7. Self-Confidence

		Describes me very well	Describes me well	Describes me fairly well	Does not describe me	Does not really describe me	Does not describe me at all
1.	Most of the time I think that the world is an exciting place to live in.	20%	33%	27%	12%	3%	5%
2.	If I put my mind to it, I can learn almost anything.	33%	32%	26%	5%	3%	2%
3.	My work, in general, is at least as good as the work of the girl/boy next to me.	12%	33%	29%	9%	17%	0%
4.	When I want something, I just sit around wishing I could have it.	6%	8%	6%	23%	42%	15%
5.	When I decide to do something, I do it.	14%	33%	34%	16%	3%	0%
6.	I find life an endless series of problems - without solution in sight.	2%	5%	0%	8%	51%	35%
7.	I feel that I am able to make decisions.	6%	59%	31%	2%	2%	0%
8.	I feel that I have no talent whatsoever.	0%	0%	6%	12%	45%	37%
9.	I am fearful of growing up.	0%	0%	3%	12%	41%	44%
10.	I repeat things continuously to be sure that I am right.	2%	20%	32%	21%	23%	3%

Scale # 8. Self-Reliance

	Describes me very well	Describes me well	Describes me fairly well	Does not describe me	Does not really describe me	Does not describe me at all
1. If I would be separated from all the people I know, I feel that I would not be able to make a go of it.	5%	9%	15%	21%	27%	23%
2. I do not like to put things in order and make sense of them.	2%	2%	5%	9%	40%	43%
3. When a tragedy occurs to one of my friends, I feel sad too.	15%	42%	34%	5%	2%	3%
4. I am a superior student at school.	2%	14%	29%	25%	20%	11%
5. Our society is a competitive one and I am not afraid of it.	15%	38%	33%	8%	2%	5%
6. I find it very difficulty to establish new friendships.	2%	2%	8%	12%	52%	26%
7. Working closely with another boy/girl never gives me pleasure.	6%	2%	8%	9%	44%	32%
8. If I know I'll be facing a new situation, I try in advance to find out as much as possible about it.	6%	49%	31%	9%	3%	2%
9. Whenever I fail in something, I try to find out what I can do in order to avoid another failure.	27%	38%	25%	6%	5%	0%
10. I am certain that I will not be able to assume responsibilities for myself in the future.	0%	3%	2%	0%	37%	59%
11. I do not rehearse how I might deal with a real coming event.	8%	5%	17%	22%	34%	15%
12. I do not enjoy solving difficult problems.	3%	11%	18%	20%	36%	12%
13. Worrying a little about one's future helps to make it work better.	9%	43%	31%	11%	5%	2%
14. Dealing with new intellectual subjects is a challenge for me.	17%	46%	24%	8%	5%	2%

Scale #9. Body Image

	Describes me very well	Describes me well	Describes me fairly well	Does not describe me	Does not really describe me	Does not describe me at all
1. The recent changes in my body have given me some satisfaction.	14%	32%	29%	14%	5%	6%
2. In the past year I have been very worried about my health.	2%	5%	9%	2%	23%	61%
3. The picture I have of myself in the future satisfies me.	32%	31%	26%	8%	2%	2%
4. I am proud of my body.	11%	39%	39%	5%	5%	2%
5. I seem to be forced to imitate the people I like.	3%	9%	17%	17%	31%	22%
6. Very often I think I am not at all the person I would like to be.	3%	11%	20%	22%	35%	9%
7. I frequently feel ugly and unattractive.	2%	3%	20%	17%	50%	8%
8. When others look at me they must think I am poorly developed.	0%	0%	2%	16%	54%	29%
9. I feel strong and healthy.	36%	38%	22%	3%	0%	2%

Scale # 10. Sexuality

	Describes me very well	Describes me well	Describes me fairly well	Does not describe me	Does not really describe me	Does not describe me at all
1. The opposite sex finds me a bore.	0%	0%	11%	15%	49%	26%
2. It is very hard for a teenager to know how to handle sex in a right way.	3%	6%	15%	23%	35%	18%
3. Dirty jokes are fun at times.	9%	8%	32%	18%	21%	12%
4. I think that girls find me attractive.	0%	17%	42%	25%	15%	2%
5. I do not attend sexy shows.	32%	25%	19%	8%	9%	8%
6. Sexually I am way behind.	0%	2%	8%	9%	48%	33%
7. Thinking or talking about sex frightens me.	0%	3%	6%	16%	39%	36%
8. Sexual experiences give me pleasure.	3%	14%	21%	27%	24%	11%
9. Having a girlfriend is important to me.	12%	24%	20%	24%	17%	3%
10. I often think about sex.	3%	20%	32%	22%	20%	3%

Scale # 11. Ethical Values

	Describes me very well	Describes me well	Describes me fairly well	Does not describe me	Does not really describe me	Does not describe me at all
1. I would not hurt someone just for the "heck of it."	51%	32%	3%	3%	2%	9%
2. I would not stop at anything if I felt I was done wrong.	3%	5%	11%	15%	32%	34%
3. I blame others even when I know that I am at fault too.	3%	5%	9%	23%	31%	29%
4. Telling the truth means nothing to me.	0%	0%	2%	2%	25%	72%
5. I do not care how my actions affect others, as long as I gain something.	2%	5%	5%	9%	39%	41%
6. For me good sportsmanship is as important as winning a game.	42%	36%	9%	6%	3%	3%
7. I like to help a friend whenever I can.	15%	57%	22%	5%	2%	0%
8. If you confide in others you ask for trouble.	2%	3%	14%	23%	39%	19%
9. Eye-for-an-eye and tooth-for-a-tooth does not apply for our society.	17%	20%	8%	24%	18%	14%
10. I would not like to be associated with kids who "hit below the belt."	31%	20%	17%	8%	15%	9%

Scale # 12. Idealism

	Describes me very well	Describes me well	Describes me fairly well	Does not describe me	Does not really describe me	Does not describe me at all
1. I am going to devote my life to helping others.	0%	5%	12%	11%	17%	56%
2. I am going to devote my life to making as much money as I can.	41%	27%	14%	0%	9%	9%
3. I am going to devote myself to making the world a better place to live in.	3%	3%	6%	14%	29%	46%
4. Even if it were dangerous, I would help someone who is in trouble.	63%	25%	8%	2%	2%	2%
5. I am against giving so much money to the poor.	5%	17%	33%	20%	22%	3%
6. There is nothing wrong with putting oneself before others.	5%	12%	34%	25%	19%	6%

Appendix C

Subjects' Hess, Henry, and Sims Identity Scale Endorsements at Age 19 (N = 52)

The positive pole sometimes appears first and sometimes appears last; a code of "1" therefore, is sometimes the most positive and a code of "7" at other times is most positive.

	% Code Used							
	1	2	3	4	5	6	7	
1. Sense of well being	18	57	11	4	9	0	0	Sense of emptiness
2. Emotionally disorganized	0	9	11	13	43	23	0	Emotionally integrated
3. Anxious	13	16	21	7	25	18	0	Secure
4. Sexually attractive	13	55	30	2	0	0	0	Sexually unattractive
5. Keeping	4	11	14	20	36	13	0	Giving
6. Unprepared	2	5	11	14	46	20	0	Ready
7. Feminine	2	2	0	7	9	75	0	Not Feminine
8. Sharing	23	36	16	7	14	4	0	Jealous
9. Sexually mature	4	11	4	21	46	14	0	Sexually immature
10. Contributing	18	48	13	11	9	0	0	Conserving
11. Willing to be a leader	34	25	21	11	7	2	0	Unwilling to be a leader
12. Foolhardy	0	5	16	18	43	18	0	Careful
13. Difficulty in sharing feelings	2	14	20	2	41	21	0	Usually express feelings Easily
14. Powerful	7	54	27	7	5	0	0	Ineffective
15. Unproductive	2	4	9	13	50	23	0	Productive
16. Unskilled	0	4	7	18	43	25	0	Skilled
17. Giving	14	41	20	9	13	2	0	Demanding
18. Clean	48	43	7	2	0	0	0	Dirty
19. Fuzzy	2	11	16	5	50	16	0	Clear
20. Willing to be a follower	5	21	32	11	16	13	0	Unwilling to be a follower
21. Contemptuous	2	5	9	23	48	9	0	Accepting
22. Justified	13	61	9	11	7	0	0	Guilty
23. Exposed and vulnerable	5	14	27	14	34	2	0	Covered and defended
24. Consistent feelings about myself	11	34	11	14	16	14	0	Inconsistent feelings about myself
25. Sufficient progress	20	43	14	5	13	5	0	Life is getting away from me
26. People know what to expect of me	14	45	13	13	11	5	0	People don't know what to expect of me
27. Bored	7	16	23	21	29	4	0	Ecstatic
28. People can trust me	48	21	5	14	9	2	0	Sometimes I let people down
29. Nonmasculine	0	2	2	2	43	45	0	Masculine
30. Moderate	20	25	20	13	18	5	0	Overdo things
31. Enriched	11	57	21	5	4	2	0	Barren
32. Worthy	21	52	13	7	7	0	0	Unworthy

(Continued)

(*Continued*)

	1	2	3	4	5	6	7	
			%	Code	Used			
33. Unloved	2	2	2	9	39	46	0	Loved
34. Stubborn	4	27	20	7	29	14	0	Cooperative
35. Short-lived relationships	5	13	11	4	46	21	0	Enduring relationships
36. Self-doubting	7	14	14	11	36	16	0	Self-assured
37. Relaxed	16	36	14	14	14	5	0	Tense
38. Sluggish	2	11	11	13	48	13	0	Quick
39. A sense of loneliness	9	16	14	9	38	14	0	A sense of belonging
40. Usually nonconforming	4	11	20	20	39	5	0	Usually conforming
41. On my guard with others	5	7	13	11	52	13	0	Trusting of other people
42. Growing	32	46	11	4	5	2	0	Stagnant
43. Frustration	7	18	32	18	23	2	0	Rapture
44. Acceptance of death	30	29	16	18	5	2	0	Fear of death
45. Undemonstrative	0	1	14	7	46	30	0	Affectionate
46. Safe	11	43	13	16	14	2	0	Apprehensive
47. Self-condemning	7	14	16	11	34	18	0	Acceptance of myself
48. Know what I want to be	14	30	5	11	11	29	0	Unsure as to what I want to be
49. Able to concentrate	13	29	14	13	25	7	0	Easily distracted
50. Despairing	2	7	9	7	45	30	0	Hoping
51. Inhibited	4	13	20	11	39	11	0	Spontaneous
52. On time	29	32	9	16	14	0	0	Late
53. Cynical	5	14	16	14	32	18	0	Believing
54. In control	20	50	13	13	5	0	0	Overwhelmed
55. Manipulated by others	4	9	13	7	43	21	0	Self-directed
56. Sharing	21	43	2	9	20	4	0	Lonely

Appendix D

Subjects' Symptom Check List 90-Revised Endorsements at Age 48 (N = 67)

How much were you distressed by:	Percent				
	Not at all	A little bit	Moderately	Quite a bit	Extremely
Headaches	49	40	5	6	0
Nervousness or shakiness inside	60	30	3	6	2
Repeated unpleasant thoughts that won't leave your mind	49	37	8	5	2
Faintness or dizziness	96	5	0	0	0
Loss of sexual interest or pleasure	60	22	9	6	0
Feeling critical of others	18	45	31	6	0
The idea that someone else can control your thoughts	79	15	5	0	2
Feeling others are to blame for most of your troubles	66	30	5	0	0
Trouble remembering things	27	55	15	3	0
Worried about sloppiness or carelessness	37	43	13	5	2
Feeling easily annoyed or irritated	21	49	25	5	0
Pains in heart or chest	88	9	3	0	0
Feeling afraid in open spaces or on the streets	94	5	2	0	0
Feeling low in energy or slowed down	18	48	28	5	2
Thoughts of ending your life	94	5	0	0	2
Hearing voices that other people do not hear	100	0	0	0	0
Trembling	94	3	3	0	0
Feeling that most people cannot be trusted	64	33	3	0	0
Poor appetite	82	10	6	2	0
Crying easily	84	13	2	2	0
Feeling shy or uneasy with the opposite sex	78	16	5	2	0
Feelings of being trapped or caught	70	25	5	0	0
Suddenly scared for no reason	88	12	0	0	0
Temper outbursts that you could not control	73	18	9	0	0
Feeling afraid to go out of your house alone	99	2	0	0	0
Blaming yourself for things	45	43	9	3	0
Pains in lower back	57	24	12	3	5
Feeling blocked in getting things done	42	31	22	2	3
Feeling lonely	55	31	8	3	3
Feeling blue	48	42	3	6	2
Worrying too much about things	30	45	18	6	2
Feeling no interest in things	69	24	6	2	0
Feeling fearful	66	28	6	0	0
Your feelings being easily hurt	61	30	6	2	2
Other people being aware of your private thoughts	81	13	3	3	0
Feeling others do not understand you or are unsympathetic	69	27	3	2	0
Feeling that people are unfriendly or dislike you	78	21	2	0	0

(Continued)

(Continued)

How much were you distressed by:	Percent				
	Not at all	A little bit	Moderately	Quite a bit	Extremely
Having to do things very slowly to insure correctness	43	48	6	3	0
Heart pounding or racing	88	9	2	2	0
Nausea or upset stomach	73	16	8	2	2
Feeling inferior to others	78	16	6	0	0
Soreness of your muscles	45	36	10	8	2
Feeling that you are watched or talked about by others	79	15	5	2	0
Trouble falling asleep	54	22	12	8	5
Having to check and double-check what you do	43	45	9	3	0
Difficulty making decisions	57	34	3	5	2
Feeling afraid to travel on buses, subways, or trains	94	6	0	0	0
Trouble getting your breath	88	9	2	2	0
Hot or cold spells	90	8	3	0	0
Having to avoid certain things, places, or activities because they frighten you	93	6	2	0	0
Your mind going blank	60	31	8	2	0
Numbness or tingling in parts of your body	73	24	3	0	0
A lump in your throat	94	3	2	2	0
Feeling hopeless about the future	67	25	5	3	0
Trouble concentrating	48	39	10	2	2
Feeling weak in parts of your body	70	19	8	2	2
Feeling tense or keyed up	28	51	13	6	2
Heavy feelings in your arms or legs	90	9	2	0	0
Thoughts of death or dying	75	19	3	2	2
Overeating	58	21	18	3	0
Feeling uneasy when people are watching or talking about you	72	18	6	2	2
Having thoughts that are not your own	93	8	0	0	0
Having urges to beat, injure, or harm someone	91	9	0	0	0
Awakening in the early morning	51	33	9	5	3
Having to repeat the same actions such as touching, counting, or washing	84	13	3	0	0
Sleep that is restless or disturbed	45	30	15	10	0
Having urges to break or smash things	85	13	2	0	0
Having ideas or beliefs that others do not share	58	30	10	0	2
Feeling very self-conscious with others	72	18	8	3	0
Feeling uneasy in crowds, such as shopping or at a movie	78	15	5	3	0

(Continued)

(Continued)

How much were you distressed by:	Not at all	A little bit	Moderately	Quite a bit	Extremely
Feeling everything is an effort	67	27	6	0	0
Spells of terror or panic	94	6	0	0	0
Feeling uncomfortable about eating or drinking in public	93	8	0	0	0
Getting into frequent arguments	87	9	5	0	0
Feeling nervous when you are left alone	93	8	0	0	0
Others not giving you proper credit for your achievements	58	28	12	2	0
Feeling lonely even when you are with people	69	22	9	0	0
Feeling so restless you couldn't sit still	70	25	5	0	0
Feelings of worthlessness	79	16	5	0	0
The feeling that something bad is going to happen to you	76	22	0	2	0
Shouting or throwing things	82	15	3	0	0
Feeling afraid you will faint in public	99	2	0	0	0
Feeling that people will take advantage of you if you let them	52	36	9	3	0
Having thoughts about sex that bother you a lot	87	9	5	0	0
The idea that you should be punished for your sins	90	8	3	0	0
Thoughts and images of a frightening nature	90	10	0	0	0
The idea that something serious is wrong with your body	76	19	3	0	2
Never feeling close to another person	81	15	2	3	0
Feelings of guilt	60	31	8	2	0
The idea that something is wrong with your mind	85	15	0	0	0

References

Block, J. (1993). Studying personality the long way. In D. Funder, R. Parke, C. Tomlinson-Keasey, & K. Widaman (Eds.), *Studying lives through time: Personality and development.* (pp. 9–41). Washington, D.C.: American Psychological Association.

Block, J. (1971). *Lives through time.* Berkley, CA: Bancroft.

Caspi, A. (2002). The cumulative continuity model of personality development: Striking a balance between continuity and change in personality traits across the life course. In U. Staudinger and U. Lindenberger (Eds.), *Understanding human development: Dialogues with lifespan psychology.* (pp. 183–214). Dordrecht, Netherlands: Kluwer Academic Publishers.

Caspi, A. (1987). Personality in the life course. *Journal of Personality and Social Psychology, 53,* 1203–1213.

Caspi, A. (1998). Personality development across the life course. In W. Damon and N. Eisenberg (Eds.), *Handbook of Child Psychology, Vol. 3: Social, emotional and personality development.* (pp. 311–388). New York: Wiley.

Caspi, A. (2000). The child is father of the man: Personality continuities from childhood to adulthood. *Journal of personality and Social Psychology, 78,* 158–172.

CDC, National center for chronic disease prevention and health promotion, 2001.

CDC, National center for health statistics, 2002.

Clausen, J. A. (1976). Glimpses into the social world of middle age. *International Journal of Aging and Human Development, 7,* 99–106.

Clausen, J. A. (1991). Adolescent competence and the life course, or why one social psychologist needed a concept of personality. *Social Psychology Quarterly, 54,* 4–14.

Clausen, J. A. (1993). *American Lives.* New York: The Free Press.

Clausen, J. A. and Jones, C. J. (1998). Predicting personality stability across the life span: The role of competence and work and family commitments. *Journal of Adult Development, 5,* 73–83.

Cohen, J. (1998, January 9), Scientists who fund themselves. *Science, 279,* 178–181.

Cohler, B. J. (1981). Personal Narrative and Life-Course. In P. Bates & O. G. Brim, Jr. (Eds.), *Life-Span Development and Behavior, 4,* (pp. 205–241). New York: Academic Press.

Cronbach, G. J. & Glaser, G. I. (1965). *Psychological tests and personal discussions.* Urbana, Il: University of Illinois Press.

Culligan, J. J. (1991). *You, too, can find anybody.* North Miami, Fl: Hallmark Press.

Derogatis, L. R. (1994). *SCL-90-R.* Minneapolis: National Computer Systems, Inc.

Douvan, E. and Adelson, J. (1966). *The adolescent experience.* New York: John Wiley and Sons, Inc.

Elder, G. H., Jr. (1974). *Children of the great depression.* Chicago: University of Chicago Press.

Erikson, E. H. (1950). *Childhood and society.* New York: W. W. Norton.

Ferraro, E. (1989). *You can find anyone!.* Santa Ana, CA: Marathon Press.

Freud, A. (1958). Adolescence. In K. Eissler (Vol. 16.), *Psychoanalytic Study of the Child* (Vol. XVI, pp. 225–278). New York: International Universities Press.

Grant, B., et al. (1992). Epidemiologic Bulletin. No. 35: Prevalence of DSM-IV alcohol abuse and dependence. *Alcohol Health & Research World, 18(3),* 243–248.

Hartmann, E. (1958). *Ego psychology and the problems of adaptation.* New York: International Universities Press.

Heath, C. W. (1945). *What People Are.* Cambridge: Harvard University Press.

Heath, D. H. (1991). *Fulfilling Lives.* San Francisco: Jossey-Bass.

Hess, R., Henry, W. E. & Sims, J. H. (1968). The Identity Scale. *The Actor.* Unpublished manuscript, University of Chicago.

Holinger, P. C. & Offer, D. (1982). Prediction of adolescent suicide: a population model. *American Journal of Psychiatry, 139,* 302–307.

Johnson, R. S. (1990). *How to locate anyone who is or has been in the military.* Ft. Sam Houston, TX: Military Information Enterprises.

Jones, H. E. (1938). The California Adolescent Growth Study. *Journal of Education Research, 31,* 561–567.

Jones, H. E. (1939a). Principles and methods. *Journal of Consulting Psychology, 3,* 157–159.

Jones, H. E. (1939b). The Adolescent Growth Study. II. Procedures. *Journal of Consulting Psychology, 3,* 177–180.

Macfarland, J. W. (1938). Some findings from a ten-year guidance research program. *Progressive Education. 7,* 529–535.

Masterson, J. F., Jr. (1967). *The psychiatric dilemma of adolesence.* Boston: Little, Brown & Company.

McAdams, D. P. (1993). *The stories we live by: Personal myths and the making of the self.* New York: Morrow.

National household survey on drug abuse, Office of applied studies, 2001.

National institute on alcohol abuse and alcoholism, 1992.

Offer, D., Ostrov, E. & Howard, K. I. (1979). *A manual for the self-image questionnaire for adolescents* (2nd ed.). Chicago, Michael Reese Hospital and Medical Center: Special Publication.

Offer, D. (1969). *The Psychological world of the teen-ager.* New York: Basic Books, Inc.

Offer, D. & Diesenhaus, H. (1969). *The Offer self-image questionnaire for adolescents—A manual.* Chicago: Special publication, Michael Reese Hospital and Medical Center.

Offer, D., Kaiz, M., Ostrov, E., and Albert, D. B. (2003). Continuity of Family Constellation. *Adolescent and Family Health, 3(1),* 3–8.

Offer, D., Kaiz, M., Howard, K. I., and Bennett, E. (2000). The Altering of Reported Experiences. *Journal of American Academy of Child and Adolescent Psychiatry, 39(6),* 735–742.

Offer, D., Offer, J. B. & Ostrov, E. (1975). *From teenage to young manhood.* New York: Basic Books.

Offer, D., Ostrov, E., Howard, K. I. & Dolan, S. (1992). *Offer self-image questionnaire, revised (osiq-r).* Los Angeles: Western Psychological Services.

Offer, D. & Sabshin, M. (1966). *Normlity.* New York: Basic Books, Inc.

Offer, D. & Sabshin, M. (1984). *Normlity and the life cycle.* New York: Basic Books, Inc.

Offer, D. & Sabshin, M. (1991). *The diversity of normal behavior.* New York: Basic Books, Inc.

Office of Applied Studies (2001). *National Household Survey on Drug Abuse.* Washington, D.C.: U.S. Department of health and Human Services.

Schacter, D. L. (2001). *The Seven Sins of Memory.* Boston: Houghton Mifflin Company.

Vaillant, G. E. (1974). The natural history of male psychological health II: Some antecedents of health adult adjustment. *Archives of General Psychiatry, 31,* 15–22.

Vaillant, G.E. (1977). *Adaptation to life.* Boston, MA: Little, Brown.

Vaillant, G. E. (1983). *The natural history of alcoholism: Causes, patterns, and paths to recovery.* Cambridge, MA: Harvard Univ. Press.

Vaillant, G. E. (1998). Natural history of male psychological health XIV: Relationship of mood disorder vulnerability to physical health. *American Journal of Psychiatry, 155,* 184–190.

Vaillant, G. E. (2000). Adaptive mental mechanisms: Their role in positive psychology. *American Psychologist, 55,* 89–98.

Vaillant, G. E. (2002). *Aging well.* New York, NY: Little, Brown.

Index